THE HANDBOOK OF DINING; OR, HOW TO DINE, THEORETICALLY, PHILOSOPHICALLY AND HISTORICALLY CONSIDERED

THE HANDBOOK OF DINING; OR, HOW TO DINE, THEORETICALLY, PHILOSOPHICALLY AND HISTORICALLY CONSIDERED

Brillat-Savarin and Leonard Francis Simpson

www.General-Books.net

Publication Data:

Title: The Handbook of Dining
Subtitle: Or, How to Dine, Theoretically, Philosophically and Historically Considered
Author: Brillat-Savarin and Leonard Francis Simpson
Reprinted: 2010, General Books, Memphis, Tennessee, USA
Publisher: Longman, Brown, Green, Longmans Roberts
Publication date: 1859
Subjects: Gastronomy
Cooking / General
Cooking / Essays
Cooking / Regional Ethnic / French
Cooking / History
Social Science / Customs Traditions
BISAC subject codes: CKB000000, CKB030000, CKB034000, CKB041000, SOC005000

How We Made This Book for You

We made this book exclusively for you using patented Print on Demand technology.

First we scanned the original rare book using a robot which automatically flipped and photographed each page.

We automated the typing, proof reading and design of this book using Optical Character Recognition (OCR) software on the scanned copy. That let us keep your cost as low as possible.

If a book is very old, worn and the type is faded, this can result in numerous typos or missing text. This is also why our books don't have illustrations; the OCR software can't distinguish between an illustration and a smudge.

We understand how annoying typos, missing text or illustrations, foot notes in the text or an index that doesn't work, can be. That's why we provide a free digital copy of most books exactly as they were originally published. You can also use this PDF edition to read the book on the go. Simply go to our website (www.general-books.net) to check availability. And we provide a free trial membership in our book club so you can get free copies of other editions or related books.

OCR is not a perfect solution but we feel it's more important to make books available for a low price than not at all. So we warn readers on our website and in the descriptions we provide to book sellers that our books don't have illustrations and may have numerous typos or missing text. We also provide excerpts from books to book sellers and on our website so you can preview the quality of the book before buying it.

If you would prefer that we manually type, proof read and design your book so that it's perfect, simply contact us for the cost. Since many of our books only sell one or two copies, we have to split the production costs between those one or two buyers.

Frequently Asked Questions

Why are there so many typos in my paperback?

We created your book using OCR software that includes an automated spell check. Our OCR software is 99 percent accurate if the book is in good condition. Therefore, we try to get several copies of a book to get the best possible accuracy (which is very difficult for rare books more than a hundred years old). However, with up to 3,500 characters per page, even one percent is an annoying number of typos. We would really like to manually proof read and correct the typos. But since many of our books only sell a couple of copies that could add hundreds of dollars to the cover price. And nobody wants to pay that. If you need to see the original text, please check our website for a downloadable copy.

Why is the index and table of contents missing (or not working) from my paperback?

After we re-typeset and designed your book, the page numbers change so the old index and table of contents no longer work. Therefore, we usually remove them. We dislike publishing books without indexes and contents as much as you dislike buying them. But many of our books only sell a couple of copies. So manually creating a new index and table of contents could add more than a hundred dollars to the cover price. And nobody wants to pay that. If you need to see the original index, please check our website for a downloadable copy.

Why are illustrations missing from my paperback?

We created your book using OCR software. Our OCR software can't distinguish between an illustration and a smudge or library stamp so it ignores everything except type. We would really like to manually scan and add the illustrations. But many of our books only sell a couple of copies so that could add more than a hundred dollars to the cover price. And nobody wants to pay that. If you need to see the original illustrations, please check our website for a downloadable copy.

Why is text missing from my paperback?

We created your book using a robot who turned and photographed each page. Our robot is 99 percent accurate. But sometimes two pages stick together. And sometimes a page may even be missing from our copy of the book. We would really like to manually scan each page. But many of our books only sell a couple of copies so that could add more than a hundred dollars to the cover price. And nobody wants to pay that. If you would like to check the original book for the missing text, please check our website for a downloadable copy.

1

THE HANDBOOK OF DINING; OR, HOW TO DINE, THEORETICALLY, PHILOSOPHICALLY...

TRANSLATORS PREFACE.

There was commotion in Olympus in January, 1859.

Venus, Minerva, and Juno whispered together so long that at last the attention of Jupiter was attracted. " What is the matter? " exclaimed the father of gods and men. " Poor little Gasterea is in a great way," said Venus eagerly, " and wishes to be admitted to an audience; Juno says she has no business here, as in her circle she gives nothing but nectar and ambrosia, and I cannot convince her that Gasterea has no intention of reforming our repasts."

Now, be it known, Venus and Gasterea have a secret treaty between them,—offensive and defensive,—in case a third power, called " Ennui," should encroach upon the territory of either. Thus, Gasterea has always a voice at the Imperial Court.

"I have not seen the child," said Jupiter, "for a long time. Show her in!"

Venus vanished, and soon reappeared, leading by the hand as fair a specimen of the demi-goddess as mortal or celestial eye ever beheld. Nearly as tall as Venus, with laughing eye, rounded limbs, golden hair, in natural waves that might make Hebe jealous, a pouting coral lip set off by teeth of pearls, she knelt at the feet of Jupiter. He raised her gently, and kissed her forehead. Juno whistled to her peacock, and left the cloud upon which she had been reclining.

The Handbook of Dining; Or, How to Dine, Theoretically, Philosophically and Historically Considered. Brillat-Savarin and Leonard Francis Simpson

1

"Speak, my child," said Jupiter, patting her cheek; " what is wrong? Whatever the cause, we are glad to see you. You are wonderfully improved: one day, perhaps, you shall have a seat here, near Venus, and a temple of your own."

Thus encouraged, Gasterea told her piteous tale:

"There is a race," she said, " of bold sea-girt islanders who worship me well in their way; indeed, mighty fires of coal never cease to burn in my honour; but it is a melancholy fact, that London does not know How To Dine !"

"Leave England alone," replied Jupiter, " it is a hospitable land, the last refuge of Liberty. If the fate of nations depends upon how they are fed, England must live well. Even now, my discerning glance can see a ship with a noble freight of patriots steering for her shores, and they will receive a hearty welcome from your island worshippers. They are a hardy and honourable race, those sons of Britain, the compensating balance of the political world."

"It is precisely on this account that I wish to improve their dinners," retorted the pert maiden. "They eat too much, and they drink too much, which is worse; and their dinners are monotonous. They want Eeform! But here is my Eeform Bill." "Which," hastily added Jupiter, "I will read at my leisure;" and he gave it to his eagle. "Meantime, what can I do to further your views?"

"Send Mercury to touch with his wand, imbued with the magic spirit of Dinner-Eeform, any one of the houses you see between these two letters," exclaimed Gasterea, pointing to W. and S. W. on the new postal district map, " and you will see the result."

"I will do more," said the father of the gods,

"he shall touch the dwelling of my great confrere, whose sway below equals mine here, and whose thunder shall be heard."

So said, so done.

Obedient to the Olympian nod, Mercury prepared for flight:

"He said; and straight, with zealous ardour prest,
Mercury prepares t obey his Lords behest.
He clothes his heavenly form with ether light,
And makes it visible to human sight;
In shape and limbs like one of earthly race,
But brightly shining with celestial grace;
Of youth he seemd in manhoods ripening years,
On the smooth cheek when first the down appears;
Eefulgent rays his beauteous looks unfold,
White are his nimble wings and edgd with gold.
With these through winds and clouds he cuts his way,
Flies oer the land and skims along the sea.
Thus stood bold Mercury, prepard for flight,
Then instant darted from th empyreal height;
Direct to London, now, his course he bent,
There closed his plumes, and made a safe descent."

On the following morning, as all our readers are aware, the columns of the London newspapers teemed with letters on dinner-giving. Like a snow-ball, the correspondence increased in volume. Public attention was aroused. Then came the deep tones of the great organ arranging into harmony the various points started as likely to promote the desired reforms.

Slightly altered from Tasso.

From North to South, from East to West, letters poured in. England was resolved to learn "How To Dine."

Gasterea was satisfied. Once again, through the interest of Venus, she was admitted to express her thanks to Jupiter. " I have still one favour to ask," said the voluptuous Queen of Gastronomy. " One of my most devoted worshippers lies huried on the hanks of the Seine. He understood me well, and out of gratitude I plant the earliest flowers on his grave. Let the shade of Savarin be invoked!"

It was done.

Brillat Savarins maxims for dining and giving dinners are now, thanks to Gasterea, placed before the Amphitryons of London in the

" Handbook Of Dining !"

London: 13th March, 1859.

PREFACE.

(conden8ed From Savarin.)

Considering the pleasures of the table under all their aspects, it struck me forcibly that the subject was worthy of something better than an ordinary cookery-book, and that there was a wide field to examine into essential and necessary functions, which have so direct an influence on the health and happiness of man, and even upon his affairs. This idea having assumed form and shape, the remainder came naturally. I looked around me, made notes; and often, in the midst of a sumptuous banquet, the pleasure of observation saved me from the ennuis of the dinner.

It is true, to carry out my idea, some knowledge of medicine, chemistry, physiology, and even a little learning was requisite. But without ever dreaming of becoming an author, I had studied those various branches in my youth, from a very praiseworthy desire of being able to converse with the various men I might meet in society, and not be behind my century.

I often entertained a doubt my book might be tedious, and make other men yawn as I often have yawned over other mens books. I have done all in my power not to deserve such a reproach. I have passed lightly over tedious subjects; the anecdotes related are in many instances personal; I have left untouched a number of extraordinary and singular facts which sound criticism rejects; I have awakened attention by making clear and popular certain facts which savans seemed inclined to reserve to themselves. If, despite these efforts, I have served up an indigestible banquet, I shall not sleep the less sound with the conscience of having earned the approbation of the majority.

I do not, however, wish to be thought a Compiler; had I been reduced so low, my pen should not have been taken up, and I should not have lived less happily on that account.

I said with Juvenal:

"Semper ego auditor tantum! nunquamne reponam."

And those who know me are aware that I am as accustomed to the tumult of society as to the privacy of the cabinet.

Finally, when I speak in the singular, "I," let the reader remember I am conversing with him, but when I make use of the pronoun "We," I profess and exact subjection:
"I am Sir Oracle, And when I ope my lips, let no dog bark."
Merchant of Venice, Act L Scene 1.
THE
HANDBOOK OF DINING.
INTEODUCTION.
As stated in the title-page, the following volume is based upon the " Physiologic du Gout," of Brillat Savarin; a work unrivalled in its peculiar sphere. Many parts are, however, condensed, others omitted, as not suited to the present tone of society. It is curious that a translation of this remarkable book has not long since been made. An article in the "Quarterly," which appeared some years since, founded, if we err not, on Savarins work, for a moment drew attention to an effusion which may be placed on the same shelf with Eousseau, Voltaire, or the political economy of Bastiat. It is, in fact, not a cookery-book; it is a brilliant treatise (as the title, "Physiologic du Gout," implies) on gastronomy or the art of eating, regarded in all its

branches. Some of the anecdotes are most amusing; some of the ideas most instructive; the work a masterpiece in its way. The art of dining is quite distinct from the art of giving dinners; but no person can read through these pages without coming to the conclusion that gastronomy is a science well worthy the study of persons of intellect of both sexes; and it will lead them to the conviction, that a little more study in the selection of their dishes, the management of their kitchen, and due attention to the comfort of their guests, will enhance tenfold the pleasures of the table, and make their dinners select.

Eeform in dinner-giving is on the tapis, and we trust it will not be dropped. A move has been made in the right direction. Savarins Aphorisms in the first chapter contain, pretty nearly, all the general rules to be observed.

There are a few passages somewhat free–but, gentle reader, skip them over–they are only poppies in a corn-field–dandelions on the same bank as the blue-eyed violet.

A brief sketch of Brillat Savarin himself may not prove uninteresting.

Anthelme Brillat Savarin was born on the 1st April, 1755, at Belley, a small town at the foot of the Alps, not far from the Ehone, where that river marks the boundary between France and Savoy. He was called to the bar at an early age, and practised with distinction. In 1789 he was returned by his fellow-citizens, member for his native place to the Constituent Assembly. He was subsequently appointed President of the Civil Tribune of the Department de 1Ain. An upright magistrate, his amiable and conciliating manners gained the esteem of all who came in contact with him. As mayor of Belley, in 1793, he boldly resisted every attempt at anarchy, and for some time warded off the Eeign of Terror from his native place. He was ultimately compelled to fly to Switzerland. He subsequently crossed the Atlantic, and spent two years at New York. He gave lessons in French to earn a livelihood, and being an excellent musician, performed nightly in the orchestra of the theatre. In after life, Brillat Savarin always recalled this period of his career with pleasure. As soon as something like quiet was restored to France, Brillat Savarin returned to his native land. He landed at Havre, in the first days of Vendemaire, year v. (September 1796).

Under thedirectory, he was employed, first, as secretary to the staff of the army of the Eepublic in Germany, afterwards as commissary of the government in the department of the Seine-et-Oise, at Versailles. He held this appointment on the 18th Brumaire.

Called to the Court of Cassation, Brillat Savarin passed the last twenty-five years of his life in that honourable calling, respected by his subordinates, enjoying the friendship of his equals, and the esteem of all who knew him. Horn/me desprit, a pleasant boon-companion, full of merriment, he was the charm of every society happy enough to possess him. In his leisure hours he wrote the " Physiologie du Gout "–to which he did not put his name. The success was immediate; the natural flow of his language won him the hearts of all readers, and the severest critics were disarmed.

Of manly and robust stature and health, Brillat Savarin himself, though he understood a good dinner, lived frugally. He caught cold at the funeral of one of his friends, and with his peculiar fine appreciation of every feeling, was at once aware that he was a dying man. The best physicians of Paris were of no avail. He died with a smile on his lips, regretted by all his friends and leaving behind him the remarkable work, which we place before the reader, as a monument to his memory. CHAPTER I.

APHOKISMS.

The universe without life would be nothing, and all that lives must be fed.

Animals feed; man eats; the man of intellect alone knows How to eat.

The fate of nations depends upon how they are fed.

IV.

Tell me what you eat, I will tell you what you are.

The Creator in making it obligatory on man to eat to live, invites him thereto by appetite, and rewards him by the pleasure he experiences.

Good living is an act of our judgment, by which we give a preference to things agreeable to taste, to those which do not possess that quality.

vn.

The pleasures of the table are for all ages, all conditions, all countries, and of great variety; they are the concomitants of all other pleasures, and when all the rest are gone, they remain to console us for their loss.

vin.

The dinner-table is the only place where men are not bored during the first hour.

The discovery of a new dish does more for the happiness of mankind, than the discovery of a new planet.

Men who eat hastily or get drunk do not know how to eat or drink.

xi.

Comestibles vary from the most substantial to the most light. (xiL.

Beverages range from the mildest to the strongest and most delicately flavoured.

xm.

To say that a man ought not to vary his wine is heresy: the palate becomes deadened; after the third glass the finest wine in the world becomes insipid.

A dinner without cheese is like a pretty woman with only one eye.

xv.

Cookery is a science. No man is born a cook.

xvI.

The. most indispensable qualification of a cook is punctuality. The same must be said of guests.

XVII.

To wait too long for a guest is a breach of politeness towards all who have arrived punctually.

A man who invites friends to dinner, and takes no personal interest in his dinner, is not worthy of friendship.

The lady of the house should always take care that the coffee is excellent; and the master of the house should be sure that the liqueurs are of the first quality.

When you invite a man to dinner, never forget that during the short time he is under your roof his happiness is in your hands.

CHAP. II.

THE PHILOSOPHICAL HISTORY OF EATING.

Cookery is the most ancient art, for Adam was born fasting, and the new-born babe that has scarcely entered the world cries until it is calmed by its mothers breast.

It is also the art which has rendered the most important service to civil society; for it is cookery which has brought into play the application of fire, and it is by fire that man has subjugated nature.

Taking a general view, cookery may be divided into three branches:

The first refers to the preparation of food, and maintains its original appellation;

The second is occupied with analysing and verifying the elements of food, and is called Chemistry;

The third, which might be called cuisine de reparation, is known under the name of Pharmacy.

If their end is different, they nevertheless are connected by the application of fire, by the use of furnaces and of the same utensils.

Thus the same piece of beef which is converted by the cook into soup or roast, is examined by the chemist to ascertain into how many substances it may be divided, whilst the apothecary cures us should it perchance be indigestible.

Man is an omnivorous animal: he has incisive teeth to eat fruit, molar teeth to mash grain, and canine teeth to tear flesh: hence the observation that man approaches nearer the savage the more his canine teeth are developed and easily discernible.

It is extremely probable that for some time the species was frugivorous from necessity, for man is the most unprotected animal of the whole world, and his means of attack limited unless armed. But the instinct of progress in-born in his nature soon developed itself: the very knowledge of his weakness induced him to fabricate weapons of defence: his carnivorous instinct represented by his canine teeth also urged him; and once armed, he preyed and fed upon all animals around him.

This instinct of destructiveness still exists; children seldom fail to kill the little animals that are left at their mercy; if they were hungry they would eatjbhem.

It is not surprising that man should have a desire to eat flesh: his stomach is too small, and fruit does not contain sufficient nourishment to satisfy him; vegetables would be better; but such a diet would imply inventions which it required centuries to perfect.

The first weapons of man were doubtless branches of trees, later bows and arrows.

It is well worthy of remark that wherever man has been discovered, no matter in what climate or what latitude, he has always been found armed with bows and arrows. It is difficult to explain this uniformity. We cannot understand how the same series of ideas should have presented itself to individuals under such different circumstances; it must proceed from a cause hidden behind the curtain of ages.

Eaw meat has one inconvenience: it sticks in the teeth: with this exception it is not disagreeable to taste; seasoned with a little salt, it digests easily, and must be more nourishing than any other food.

"Mein Qott!" said a captain of Croats to me in 1815, whom I had invited to dinner, "why so much trouble about a repast? When we are on scout-duty and are hungry, we shoot the first animal that crosses our path, we cut off a slice to our liking, sprinkle a little salt and pepper on it, of which we always carry a provision in our sabre-tasche, we place it under the saddle on the horses back, set off at a hand gallop, and (making the movement of a man tearing meat with his teeth) gnian, gnian, gnian, we dine like princes."

In the Dauphine, if a sportsman shoots a corncrake, he plucks it, rubs it inside with salt and pepper, carries it in his cap, and, when hungry, eats it. They maintain that it is much better eating thus than roasted.

Moreover, if our great-grandfathers did eat their food raw, we have not yet quite given up the habit. The most delicate palate will eat dried sausages, smoked beef and ham, anchovies, dried herrings that have never been on the fire, and like them all the same.

As soon as the properties of fire were discovered, the instinct of perfection made man apply it to food; first to dry it, then by placing it on hot embers, to cook it.

Flesh thus handled was found better; it had more consistency, was more easily chewed, and the osmazome (essence of the meat) becoming fluid, gave it a savoury flavour which was pleasing to the palate.

However, it was soon discovered that meat grilled on coals was not free from being soiled, as a portion of cinder generally adhered to it. This was remedied by sticking it on skewers, which were placed on raised stones at a sufficient height to prevent contact with the embers. This was the origin of the gridiron, a most simple and excellent invention, because the meat thus cooked always retains its flavour.

In Homers days matters were not much more advanced. Behold how Achilles received three of the noblest amongst the Greeks, one of whom was a king:—

"With that, the Chiefs beneath his roof he led,
And plac'd in seats with purple carpets spread.
Then thus:–Patroclus, crown a larger bowl,
Mix purer wine, and open every soul.
Of all the warriors yonder host can send,
Thy friend most honours these, and these thy friend.
He said; Patroclus oer the blazing fire,
Heaps in a brazen vase three chines entire:
The brazen vase Automedon sustains,
Which flesh of porkct, sheep, and goat contains:
Achilles at the genial feast presides,

The parts transfixes, and with skill divides.
Meanwhile Patroclus sweats the fire to raise;
The tent is lightend with the rising blaze:
    Then, when the languid flames at length subside,
He throws a bed of glowing embers wide,
Above the coals the smoking fragments turns,
And sprinkles sacred salt from lifted urns.
With bread the glittering canisters they load,
Which round the board Mencetius son bestowd;
Himself opposed t Ulysses full in sight,
Each portion parts, and orders every rite.
The first fat offerings, to th Immortals due,
Amidst the greedy flames Patroclus threw;
Then each, indulging in the social feast,
His thirst and hunger soberly represt.
That done, to Phoenix Ajax gave the sign;
Not unperceivd; Ulysses crownd with wine
The foaming bowl, and instant thus began,
His speech addressing to the god-like man:
Health to Achilles," andc.
    Iliad, Canto IX. Popes Translation.
    That Achilles and Patroclus should themselves have prepared the repast, is an exceptional case out of honour to their illustrious guests, for the duties of the kitchen generally fell to the lot of the women and slaves.
    Here we have the fact of a king, the son of a king, and three Greek generals making an excellent dinner on bread, wine, and a grill.
    The bowels of animals, stuffed with blood and fat, formed a favourite dish of the Greeks. It was nothing more than sausage.
    At this period, and doubtless long before, poetry and music were associated with the pleasures of the table. Venerable bards sang the wonders of nature, the loves of the gods, and the noble deeds of warriors; they formed a sort of priesthood, and it is not impossible that the divine Homer himself may have been the issue of one of those favoured men of Heaven; he could not have attained so high a position if his poetical studies had not commenced in his childhood.
    Madame Dacier observes that Homer never speaks of boiled beef in any portion of his work. The Hebrews were more advanced, owing to their sojourn in Egypt; they had cooking utensils which they placed on the fire, and it was in such a utensil that Jacob made the mess of porridge he sold so dear to his brother Esau.
    It is difficult to ascertain how man first learnt to forge metal. I have never been able to ascertain how the first pair of pincers and the first hammer were fabricated.
    Cookery made a great step in advance as soon as vessels of metal or of clay could be fabricated to resist the action of fire. It became easy to season meat, to boil vegetables; soup, gravy, jelly became the natural results consequent thereon.
    The most ancient writers speak of the banquets of the kings of the East. It is easily imagined that monarchs reigning over lands rich in every produce, especially in

perfumes and spices, should maintain a sumptuous table; but details are wanting. We only know that Cadmus, who introduced the art of writing into Greece, was formerly cook to the King of Sidon.

It was amongst these voluptuous and sensual i rulers that was first introduced the custom of lying on beds round the dinner-table, and of eating in a recumbent posture.

This refinement was not universally well received. The more warlike nations, who prized manly courage and looked upon frugality as a virtue, rejected it for a long time; but it was finally adopted at Athens and in the civilised world.

The Athenians, men of elegant taste and eager for novelty, soon became adepts in the art of cookery. Kings, poets, financiers, litterateurs, made most of the bountiful gifts of nature.

If we are to credit ancient writers, their banquets were great festivals. Fish and game were always to be had, though the demand made prices run high. Eeclining on couches covered

with purple, every art was brought into requisition to satisfy the senses. The good cheer was heightened by agreeable converse, and dining became a science. After the third course singers were introduced, and conversation relaxed. The songs were not exclusively devoted to the gods and heroes; more tender subjects were introduced; love and friendship were sung with a harmony to which our diy and severe language can never attain. The wines of Greece, which we still esteem as excellent, had been examined and classified by the gourmets of the day, from the sweetest to the strongest. At some banquets each wine was passed in succession, and, contrary to modern taste, the size of the glasses increased in proportion to the quality of the wine poured out.

Beautiful women added a charm to these voluptuous meetings. Dances and games enlivened the evening. Attractions attacked every sense; many a disciple of Plato left under the banner of Epicurus.

Learned men devoted their pen to describe these enjoyments. Most of their writings are lost, but one is most to be regretted—a book on gastronomy by Achestrades, a friend of one of the sons of Pericles.

"That great writer (says Theotimus) travelled by land and sea to discover where what was most delicate for the table was produced. In his travels he did not attempt to change the customs of the people, because he knew it would be labour lost, but he entered their kitchens, and only visited men devoted to pleasure. His poem is a gem of science, and every line a precept."

Such was the state of cookery in Greece, which was maintained until a handful of men who had settled on the banks of the Tiber spread their dominion, first over their neighbours, and finally conquered the world.

Good cheer was unknown or discarded by the Eomans as long as they had to fight for their independence or to conquer their neighbours, poor and hardy like themselves. Their generals did not disdain to put their hand to the plough or to dine off vegetables.

Historians are not wanting who have praised those primitive times when frugality was deemed a virtue. But when their conquests extended to Africa, to Sicily, to Greece,—when they had regaled themselves at the expense of the vanquished, in lands where civilisation was more advanced,—they translated to Eome what had pleased them in foreign parts, and there is every reason to believe that the new introductions were well received.

The Eomans had sent a deputation to Athens to bring back the laws of Solon. They went again to study literature and philosophy. Whilst polishing their manners, they became acquainted with the pleasures of the table; and with orators, philosophers, rhetoricians, and poets–Cooks arrived at Eome.

In time, when Eome became the centre of the riches of the world, the luxury of the table was carried to a degree almost incredible. From the locust to the ostrich, from the dormouse to the wild boar, everything was tasted. " Glires isicio porcino, item pulpis ex omni glirium membro tritis, cum pipere, nuclseis, lasere, liquamine, farcies glires, et sutos in tegula positos, mittes in furnum, aut farsos in clibaro coques."

The dormouse was esteemed as a delicacy. Sometimes scales were placed on the table to verify its weight. Martial wrote an epigram on the subject,–

"Tota mihi dormitur hyems, et pingnior illo
Tempore sum, quo me nil nisi somnus alit."

The whole world was placed under contribution by armies and travellers. Truffles and guinea-fowls were imported from Africa, rabbits from Spain, pheasants from Greece, and peacocks from the remotest parts of Asia.

The opulent Eomans vied with each other in the glory of having beautiful gardens, where they cultivated not only the fruits formerly known, as apples, pears, figs and grapes, but fruits introduced from foreign lands, as the apricot from Armenia, the peach from Persia, the quince from Sidon, strawberries from the valleys of Mount Ida, and the cherry the conquest of Lucullus in Pontus. These importations, which necessarily took place under various circumstances, prove, at least, that the impulse was general, and that every man had it at heart to contribute to the enjoyments of the people-king.

Fish was an especial object of luxury. Preferences were established for certain sorts; and those preferences increased for fish caught in certain waters. Fish from distant lands was brought to Home in pots of honey;. and when the specimens were of unusual dimensions, they fetched enormous prices, in consequence of the competition of individuals many of whom were richer than kings.

Nor was less care bestowed on beverages. The wines of Greece, of Sicily, of Italy were the delight of the Eomans; and, as their price varied either according to the vineyard or the year of vintage, a sort of certificate of birth was engraven on each amphora.

"O nata mecum consule Manlio."–Hor.

This was not all. In consequence of this instinct of improvement already alluded to, attempts were made to render the wine more perfumed and delectable by the infusion of fruits, flowers and spices (cups); and the preparations which writers of the period have transmitted to us under the name of condita must have been hot to the mouth and have irritated the stomach.

Thus, already, at that distant period, the Eomans dreamt of alcohol, which was not discovered till nearly fifteen centuries later.

But it was chiefly in the accessories of the repasts that this gigantic luxury was carried to an extreme.

All the furniture requisite for the banquet was of costly material or exquisite workmanship. The number of. courses was gradually increased till it exceeded twenty; and after each course everything which had served for the previous course was removed and fresh supplied.

Slaves were specially appointed to each convivial function, and those functions were most minutely defined. The most delicious perfumes embalmed the banquet-hall. A master of the ceremonies announced the merit of the dishes most worthy of special attention–the claims they possessed to this sort of ovation; finally, nothing was omitted of a nature to sharpen the appetite, keep alive the attention, and prolong enjoyment.

This luxury had also its follies and absurdities. Such were those banquets where the fishes and birds served counted by thousands, and those dishes which had no other merit than that of having cost an enormous price, such as that dish which consisted of the brains of 500 ostriches, and that other of the tongues of 5000 birds, all -of which had been taught to speak.

After the above the enormous sums spent by Lucullus at his banquets, and the cost of the feasts he gave in the hall of Apollo, will be readily understood. At these feasts the etiquette was to exhaust every known means to flatter the sensuality of the guests.

Those glorious days might be revived at our own time, but we want a Lucullus. Let us sup pose some man known to be enormously rich, desirous of celebrating a great political or financial event, and of giving on the occasion a memorable festival without regard to expense.

Let us suppose that he engages the service of every art to adorn the place of the festival in every detail; that he gives orders that recourse be had to every means to procure the rarest provisions and the noblest wines of the most famed cellars;

That he has a troupe of the first actors of the day to perform for the amusement of his guests;

That the banquet be enlivened by vocal and instrumental music, performed by the first artistes of the day;

That, as an entracte, between dinner and coffee, a ballet performed by the best and prettiest dancers shall enliven his guests;

That the evening shall close with a ball, at which two hundred women, selected amongst the most beautiful, and four hundred elegant dancers shall attend;

That the buffet be provided with the most excellent hot and cold beverages, fresh and iced;

That at midnight a wisely selected collation shall imbue new life into all;

That the servants be handsome and well-dressed, the illumination perfect, and, moreover, that the Amphitryon should have arranged for every guest to be sent for and conveyed home without discomfort;–the bill on the following day might startle even the cashier of Lucullus, as will be readily admitted by all who are well acquainted with Paris.

What was first done by the Athenians, afterwards by the Eomans, and at a later period in the middle ages by ourselves, and at a still more recent period, is to be attributed to the nature of man, who impatiently strives to exhaust the career upon which he has entered, and to a sort of anxiety which torments him as long as the sum total of life he has at his disposal is not filled up.

Like the Athenians, the Eomans ate in a reclining position, but they only adopted it by degrees. They first made use of couches for repasts offered to the gods; the high dignitaries of the state and men in power then adopted the habit; it soon became general, and was maintained until near the beginning of the fourth century of the Christian era.

These couches, which were at first little more than stuffed seats of skins and straw, soon partook of the luxury appertaining to these feasts. The most costly wood was used, inlaid with gold and ivory, and often with precious stones; the cushions were of the softest down, and the richest stuffs covered them.

At dinner you reclined on your left side, leaning on your elbow; and generally the same couch held three persons.

Was this mode of dining, called by the Eomans lecti-stemium, more comfortable or pleasant than that which we have adopted, or rather resumed? Ve do not think so.

Physically considered, the recumbent posture exacts a certain exertion to keep an equilibrium, and the weight of the body on the arm causes a certain amount of discomfort.

There is also something to be said in a physiological point of view; the food is not swallowed so easily, and the position of the body is not so favourable to digestion.

As regards drinking, it is still more inconvenient, and it required some skill not to spill the wine from the large cups which were in use at great houses, and it was doubtless at the time of the lecti-sternium that the proverb arose:–

"There is many a slip from the cup to the lip."

Nor was it particularly clean to eat in such lying posture. The beard was worn long, and as forks were not used, but the fingers, or at most a knife, to convey the food to the mouth, it made it still more difficult. Forks are comparatively a modern invention; none were found in the ruins of Herculaneum, though spoons were found in considerable number.

It may also be presumed that a couch holding three persons, at times of both sexes, when intemperance was not unusual, did not lead to an improvement of morals, and it was not unusual for some of the guests to fall asleep.

"Nam pransus jaceo, et satur supinus
Pertundo, tunicamque, palliumquc."

As soon as Christianity established itself from the persecutions it had to suffer, its ministers raised their voice against the excesses of intemperance. They declaimed against the length of the repasts, and denounced all voluptuous indulgences. Devoted by free choice to an austere life, they placed gluttony in the list of capital sins, and the reclining posture at dinner was protested against as one of the sources of immorality and intemperance.

Their threatening voice was hearkened to: couches gradually disappeared from the banquet-room; the sitting posture was resumed, and, by rare good fortune, this posture which morality has ordained is not detrimental to pleasure.

At the period of which we write convivial poetry underwent a change, and the verse of Horace, Tibullus, and other poets of the day, breathed a voluptuousness unknown to the Greek muse.

"Dulce ridentem Lalagem amabo
Dulce loquentem."–Horace.

"Quferis quot milii basiationes
Tuse, Lesbia, sint satis superque."–Catullus.

"Pande, puella, pandc capillulos
Flavos, lucentes, ut aurum nitidum."

"Pande, paella, collum candidum
Productum bene candidis humeris."–Gallus.

The five or six centuries we have thus briefly reviewed were the great days of cookery, as well as for those who knew how to enjoy good-living. But the invasion of Barbarians from the north completely upset the art, and those glorious days of feasting were followed by a long and terrible obscurity.

As the barbarians gained ground the culinary art disappeared, with the other sciences of which it is the companion and the consoler. All the good cooks were massacred in the kitchens of their noble masters. Some fled sooner than serve men who could not appreciate their dishes. Some offered their services, but finding that these brutes had no palate for good cheer, died of grief or committed suicide. Huge roasts of beef and venison, buckets of strong drink, were quaffed by the new comers, and as every man bore weapons, blood was often shed at their banquets.

However, the very nature of things could not allow this to last. The victors became acquainted with the vanquished and ceased to be cruel; they gradually became more civilised and learnt to eat like gentlemen. Their dinners became more respectable. Men were asked not to stuff themselves but to enjoy their food; the guests discovered that the host took some pains to entertain them; they felt a pleasant contentment, and their better feelings expanded.

This improvement took place about the fifth century of our era, but a more marked improvement took place under Charlemagne; and history informs us that that great monarch took a personal interest that his domains should be well stored with game best suited to-the table.

Under Charlemagne dinners assumed a gallant and chivalrous aspect. Fair ladies embellished his court; they awarded prizes to the brave; the pheasant was served up with his golden claws, and the peacock with his magnificent tail was brought in and placed on the table of princes by pages in rich liveries of gold, and by gentle virgins whose innocence heightened their charms.

This is the third time, be it observed, that women–the greatest ornament of society– excluded from public by the Greeks, Eomans, and Franks, were admitted to table. The Turks alone have resisted the appeal. But that unsociable race cannot last, and the emancipation of sultanas is simply a question of time.

The impetus once given it has lasted down to the present day, increasing from generation to generation.

Women, even of the highest rank, did not think it beneath their dignity to oversee their kitchens, and the duties of hospitality became as sacred as they were in France at the end of the 17th century.

Under their pretty fingers some of the dishes assumed fantastic appearances. The eel was served up in the form of a serpent, the hare with the ears of a cat. Spices brought by the Venetians from the East and perfumed waters from Arabia were in great resort. It was not unusual to boil fish in rose-water. The luxury of the table consisted, in a great measure, in abundance. This was carried to such an extreme that kings found it necessary to enact laws to curtail the expense of the sumptuous banquets given; laws which were of course laughed at and ridiculed, as they were in Greece and Rome. They, however, remain as historical documents.

Good-living was kept up in monasteries and convents, especially where there were rich abbots, as from their mask of sanctity they were less exposed to interference.

Science advanced. The Crusaders brought garlic from Ascalon. Parsley was imported from Italy, and long before the reign of Louis XIV. pork and sausage-mongers made fortunes. Pastry cooks also did a good business. They had a guild of their own as far back as Charles IX., and were no contemptible body.

It may not be out of place to mention here that at Venice the luxury displayed by the nobles in their gondolas caused an order to be issued by the " Council of Ten," prohibiting all display. Some of the gondolas were studded with jewels, the oars gilt, and the money spent threatened to ruin the Republic. The Council of Ten was not to be trifled with. At the present day the gondolas at Venice resemble coffins or water-hearses.

About the middle of the 17th century the Dutch introduced coffee into Europe. Soliman Aga, that powerful Turk of whom our great-greatgrandfathers were never tired of speaking, mixed the first cups for them in 1660. An American sold coffee publicly at the fair of St. Germain in 1670: and the Eue St. Andre aux Arts opened the first coffee-shop, with marble tables and mirrors, much in the same style as the cafes of the present day.

It was about the same time that sugar was introduced!; and Scarron, when he complains that, his sister had from stinginess caused the holes of

Amongst the Europeans the Dutch were the first who imported samples of the coffee-plant from Asia to Batavia, from whence they brought it to Europe. M. de Reissont, Lieutenant-General of Artillery, had a plant sent to Amsterdam, and mada it a present to the Jardin du Roi; it is the first seen at Paris. This tree, which is described by M. Jussieu, had one inch diameter in 1613, and was five feet high; the fruit was pretty, something resembling a cherry.

f Whatever Lucretius may hare written to the contrary, sugar was unknown to the ancients. Sugar is an artificial production, and without crystallisation the cane would give a liquid insipid and of little use.

.x his sugar-box to be made smaller, informs us at least that such an article of furniture was in use at his day.

Again, it was in the 17th century that brandy commenced to be of common use. Distillation, the first idea of which was brought to Europe by the Crusaders, had hitherto remained a secret to all except a few adepts. Towards the commencement of the reign of Louis XIV. stills became common; but it was not till the reigii of Louis XV. that brandy became a popular beverage.

Tobacco also became of ordinary use nearly at the same time; so that sugar, coffee, brandy, and tobacco, those four important articles to com-. merce and the exchequer, date scarcely two centuries back.

The century of Loiiis XIV. commenced under these auspices, and in his brilliant reign the science of banquets obeyed that progressive impulse which made all other sciences advance.

The memoiy of the festivities which attracted all Europe, and those tournaments where for the last time lances were broken, now replaced by the bayonet, and those chivalrous suits of armour but a feeble defence against modern artillery, is still extant.

All those festivals terminated with sumptuous banquets, which crowned the whole; for man is so constituted that he is never happy unless his taste is gratified; and this imperious want has subjugated even grammar, for if we wish to say a thing has been done with perfection, we say it has been done with taste.

As a necessary consequence, the men who presided over the preparations of those festivities became men of note, and deservedly so; for it was requisite they should combine many qualities; the genius of invention, the tact of arrangement, the judg-ment of disposal, the sagacity to distinguish, a strong will to enforce obedience, and punctuality, so as not to keep men waiting.

It was on these great occasions that the magnificence of " plate " was introduced. Painting and sculpture played their part, the table offered a pleasing aspect to the eye; and often the site selected was appropriate to the event, or to the hero of the fete.

Here all the art and skill of the cook was set forth; but soon small dinner parties of fewer guests, and more recherche wants, exacted greater care and more minute attention.

It was at the "petit convert" in the Salon D des Favorites, and at the delicate suppers of courtiers and financiers, that artists displayed their skill, and, animated by a praiseworthy emulation, endeavoured to surpass each other.

Towards the end of this reign, the names of the most famous cooks were nearly always annexed to those of their patrons: the latter were vain of their cooks; the merits of both became united; and the most glorious names of history are to be found in cookery-books, by the side of the dishes jl they patronised, invented, or made the fashion.

This amalgamation no longer exists. We are not less gourmands than our ancestors; on the contrary; but we care much less about the name of the man who presides in the lower regions of the kitchen. Approval, by a gentle inclination of the left ear, is the only tribute of admiration which we grant to the artist that delights us; and restaurateurs, who are the cooks of the public, alone obtain a nominal esteem, which promptly places them in the rank of great capitalists. Utile dulci.

It was Louis XIV. who had the Epine dete—la bonne poire—as he called it, brought from the East; and it is to his old age that we are in debted for liqueurs.

This Prince had occasional fits of weakness, and that difficulty to live which so often manifests itself after sixty. Brandy, mixed with sugar and perfumes, was administered to him in potions he called " Cordial potions." This was the origin of liqueurs.

It may be observed, that about this same period the culinary art flourished at the Court of England. Queen Anne was fond of good cheer. She did not think it beneath her dignity to converse with her cook; and English cookery-books contain many dishes " after Queen Annes fashion."

The culinary science, which remained stationary during the sway of Madame de Maintenon, rose under the Eegency.

The Duke of Orleans, a spirituel Prince, / worthy of friendship, invited his friends to repasts as delicate as they were well selected. From the most authentic sources we learn that the most delicate piqufa, matelottes as tasty as on the rivers banks, and turkeys gloriously truffled, were the favourites.

Truffled turkeys!!! the reputation and price of which is always on the increase! Brilliant planets, whose appearance made the eyes glisten, and the lips smack of gourmands of every grade.

The reign of Louis XV. was not less favourable to the alimentary art. Eighteen years of peace soon healed the wounds of sixty years war; riches, the fruit of industry, spread by trade, in a great measure equalised fortunes; and a spirit of conviviality spread through all branches of society.

It was at this period that more order, neatness, elegance, and those various refinements were introduced, which have always gradually been increasing, and threaten at times to become ridiculous.

According to correct information which I have gathered in various provinces, a dinner of ten persons, in 1740, was as follows:–

First Course.

Soup.

Boiled beef (bouitti).

Entree de Veau cuit dans son jus.

A side dish.

Second Course.

A Turkey.

A dish of vegetables.

A salad.

A cream (sometimes).

Dessert

Cheese.

Fruit.

Sweets.

Plates were only changed thrice: viz., after the soup, at the second course, and at dessert.

Coffee was rarely given, but cherry brandy generally.

Bachelors and courtisanes kept good cooks in this reign, and did much for the art.

It is easy enough to give a large banquet to a crowd of hungry men. Beef, game, fish, poultry can be cooked wholesale and satisfy their cravings But it is a very difficult thing to gratify mouths that only nibble, to satisfy a delicate womans palate, to create a feeling in a papier mache stomach, and to excite an appetite which flickers in the socket. It requires genius, discernment, and great labour to solve one of the most difficult problems of the geometry of the indefinite.

We now come to the days of Louis XVI. and the revolution. We shall not dwell upon changes which many of us have witnessed, but shall confine ourselves to point out generally the various improvements introduced at banquets since 1774.

Those improvements belong in some measure to the natural department of the art and to the customs and social usages connected therewith; and although these two orders of things continually react upon each other, we think it as well to take each separately.

Every trade connected with the sale or preparation of food, as cooks, traiteurs, pastry-cooks, confectioners, eating-houses, andc., has increased in an ever increasing ratio. And this proves that the demand is equal to the supply.

Physics and chemistry have been called in to the aid of the alimentary art. The most learned men have not thought it beneath them to devote their attention to our primary wants, and have introduced improvements from the simple stew to the most recherche dishes which are only served up in gold or crystal. New branches of trade have arisen–biscuit bakers, for instance, who hold a middle path between pastry-cooks and confectioners. Their domain comprises butter mixed with sugar and eggs, as biscuits, buns, meringues, andc.

The art of preserving food has also become a distinct branch, the object of which is to offer us at every time of the year the various delicacies of every season.

Horticulture has made immense progress; hothouses provide us with fruits of the tropics; amongst others, the cultivation of melons is a great gain to the table.

Wines are better selected. We begin with Madeira, drink Bordeaux between the courses, and finish with port and sherry.

Caviar, soy, and other sauces are improvements meriting mention.

Coffee has become popular. It is very good for breakfast; and after dinner is exhilarating, as well as a tonic.

The word " gastronomy" is now. universally adopted, and this Greek word brings a glow of pleasure to every face. Voracity is obsolete, and your real dining-man now takes his place by the side of other artists.

Dejeuners a la fourchette are pretty repasts; they are elegant and pleasant, and a certain freedom of toilette adds to their charm.

Tea-parties are an absurdity. What does a man care for a cup of tea who has had his dinner and coffee? He is neither hungry nor thirsty. It is an excuse for receiving guests.

Political dinners have an object. They ought to be the very best in materials. They leave an impression, and " answer " at times.

The institution of " restaurateur " deserves a separate chapter.

A man with a few pounds in his pocket may now dine like a king.

CHAP. III.

DININO-HOUSES, OR RESTAURATEURS.

About the year 1770, after the glorious days of the-reign of Louis XIV., the roueries of the Ee-gency and the long tranquillity of the ministry of Cardinal Fleury, travellers arriving at Paris had but few places where they could get a good dinner. They had to put up at hotels, generally bad. A few had table-dhotes, which however only just offered what was necessary for a meal, and moreover were at fixed hours.

There were a few"traiteurs," but they had usually nothing but joints; and a man who wished to give a dinner to his friends, was obliged to order it beforehand; so that men who had not the good luck to have an introduction into opulent houses, had to leave the capital without becoming acquainted with the resources and delicacies of a Parisian kitchen.

At last a man of intellect was found who took the subject into consideration; he argued that, as the same wants occurred at about the same hour every day, men would not fail to come, if they found they were readily and well served; that if one man had a wing of chicken, the next comer would take the leg, and so on; that a slice from a prime joint would not spoil the remainder, and that a man who found he got a good dinner, would not grumble at a little expense, if promptly served, and well waited upon; and that a carte, with fixed prices for every dish, would be suitable to all fortunes. This man did not stop short here, but developed his idea still further. He was the first restaurateur, and created a profession which leads to fortune whenever the professor is honest, and combines order with skill.

From France, restaurateurs soon spread to the rest of Europe. The institution is one of extreme advantage to every citizen, and of high importance to science.

A man can now dine at any hour he pleases, according to his appetite and his means. He needs not dread his bill, as he. knows beforehand the price of each dish which he orders.

Having consulted his purse, the diner may make an excellent dinner, heavy, or light, or tasty, as lie feels inclined; he may wash it down with the generous wines of France or Spain, crown it with aromatic mocha and perfumed liqueurs, with no other restrictions than the capacity of his stomach. The salon of a restaurateur is the Eden of gourmands.

It is also very convenient for travellers, strangers, or for those whose families are out of town, who have no cook of their own.

Before the period of which we speak (1770), men of fortune or in power enjoyed, almost exclusively, two great privileges; they travelled fast and always had good cheer.

The first privilege has been done. away by railways, and the institution of restaurateurs has destroyed the second: thanks to them, good living has become universal.

Any man with fifteen francs or a pound in his pocket, who takes his seat at a table at one of the first restaurateurs, will have a better and more comfortable dinner than if he dined at the table of a prince; his dishes are as well cooked, and he is not bothered by any personal considerations.

The salon of a restaurateur, examined a little in detail, offers to the scrutinising eye of the phi losopher a picture worthy to excite an interest on account of the various phases it presents. One end is occupied by the usual crowd of daily diners, who order in a loud voice, wait impatiently, eat hastily, pay, and go. Some travelling families may be seen who, content with a frugal repast, nevertheless, generally have some dish which is new to them, which gives a zest to their dinner, and seem always to enjoy the novelty of the scene.

Next to them a Parisian couple may be seen, easily recognisable by the bonnet and shawl hung up above them. It is quite clear they have had nothing to say to each other for a long time; they have made up their mind to go to one of the minor theatres, and a man might bet any sum that one of them will go to sleep there.

Not far from them, behold a pair of lovers; the eager politeness of the one, and sly coquetry of the other, and the gourma/ndise of both betrays them. Their eyes sparkle with pleasure; and by the selection of their dishes, the present serves to pour-tray the past, and predicts the future.

In the centre there is a table, where the same men generally dine daily, at a fixed price to suit them. They know all the waiters by name, who familiarly tell them of any good dish on the table; they are like so many tame ducks, put there as decoys, to catch the wild ones.

Individuals are always to be seen there who are known to every one by sight, but whose name nobody knows. They seem perfectly at home, and often try to enter into conversation with their neighbours. They belong to a genus which exists only at Paris, and who, without property, capital, or profession, nevertheless spend a great deal of money.

Scattered about are strangers, chiefly Englishmen. These latter cram themselves with double portions, ask for all the dearest dishes, wash them down with strong wine, and do not always leave particularly steady on the legs. This picture may be daily witnessed; it may excite curiosity, perhaps even offend morality.

Doubtless the display of delicacies may induce many to exceed their means. Some delicate stomachs may experience indigestion, and Venus may make a few victims. But the dark side, as regards social life, is that there can be no doubt that dining alone leads to selfishness. A man gradually thinks of no one but himself, cares for none else; nor does he wish to be cared about; and a very little discernment is necessary, at a dinner party, to point out the men who usually dine at a restaurateurs.

We said that the institution of restaurateurs was of high importance to science.

In fact, as soon as experience proved that a single well made ragout sufficed to make the fortune of an inventor, interest, that powerful agent, fired the imagination, and sharpened the wits of the purveyors.

Analysis discovered esculent properties in substances formerly discarded as useless; new articles of food were discovered; ancient ones were improved, and both were combined in a variety of ways. Foreign inventions were imported; the universe was placed under contribution; and we have seen dinners which might have provided the material for a whole course of alimentary geography.

There are a few names deserving of historical mention as restaurateurs; Beauvilliers, Meot, Eobert, Eose, Legacque, Very, Henneveu, and Baleine. Some of them owe their reputation to peculiar dishes. The Freres Provenfaux made a fortune on cod-fish with garlic; Very was strong

This dish would scarcely have pleased Horace. Vide Ode to Maecenas:–

"Parentis olim, si qnis impia manu

Senile guttur frcgerit;

Edit cicutis alliurn nocentius."–Epodon L. c. III.

in truffles; Eobert, with due notice, would serve up a first-rate dinner; Baleine had the best fish in Paris; Henneveu had mysterious private rooms on the fourth story. But of all these heroes of gastronomy, Beauvilliers, who died in 1820, is most deserving of mention.

Beauvilliers commenced business in 1782. He was the first who had a decent dining-house. In 1814 and 1815, when Paris was occupied by the allies, carriages of every description might be seen waiting at his door. He was personally acquainted with all the foreign ambassadors, and spoke to them all in their own tongue.

Beauvilliers published, shortly before his death, a work in two volumes octavo, entitled "The Culinary Art." That work is the fruit of long experience, and is still consulted as a valuable work. Until then the culinary art had never been treated with so much precision and method. This work, which has gone through many editions, has been the groundwork of many others, but none have ever surpassed it.

Beauvilliers was gifted with a prodigious memory; after an absence of twenty years he would recognise and welcome men who had dined perhaps only once or twice in his house. At times he had a custom peculiar to himself. When he knew that a company of rich men were dining together in his salon, he would present himself, pay his respects to them, point out the best dishes to them, tell them which dish ought to be eaten first, andc. He would then send up some dish unknown to them, and a bottle of wine from his own private cellar, of which he alone kept th6 key. All this was done with so much courtesy that it appeared that these little extras were gratuitous. But this part of the Amphitryon was only momentary; he soon vanished, and the addition to the bill and bitterness of the " quart dheure" of Eabelais sufficiently convinced the guests that they had been dining at a restaurateurs.

Beauvilliers made, spent, and remade his fortune more than once. Whether he died rich or poor is not known, but he had so many calls upon him it is not likely he left a large inheritance.

The examination of the carte at a first-rate restaurateurs will show that the man who enters to dine has the choice for his dinner of at least:– 12 soups. 12 of pastry.

24 hors doeuvre. 24 of fish.

15 or 20 entrees of beef. 15 roasts.

20 entrees of mutton. 50 entremets.

30 entrees of game or fowl. 50 of dessert.

16 or 20 of veal.

Moreover, the happy gastronome may wash it down with a selection from thirty wines, from Burgundy to Tokai;–he can select from some twenty different sorts of perfumed liqueurs, without mentioning coffee, punch, and other mixtures,

A good dinner at Paris is a cosmopolitan wonder. France provides fowls and fruits, and each country of the world gives an idea or an article. Beefsteaks a langlaise, sauer kraut from Germany; wild boar from the Black Forest; an olla-podrida from Spain, garbancos and dried raisins from Malaga, hams au poivre de Xerica, and liqueurs; from Italy, macaroni, parmesan, Bolognese sausages, polenta, ices, liqueurs; from Eussia, smoked eels and caviar; dried herrings, curapoa, and anisette, from Holland; rice, sago, karisk, soy, wine of Schiraz, and coffee from Asia; Cape wine from Africa; ananas, sugar, and other eatables from America.

CHAP. IV.

THE SENSES.

The senses are the organs by which man is brought into contact with external objects.

Sight, which embraces space and informs us, through the medium of light, of the existence and of the colour of the bodies which surround us.

Hearing, which receives, through the intermedium of the air, the vibration caused by noisy or sonorous bodies.

Smell, by the means of which we appreciate the odour of bodies that possess it.

Taste, by which we appreciate everything sapid or esculent.

Touch, the object of which is the consistency and surface of bodies.

If we may be allowed to carry back our imagination to the first moments of the existence of the human species, we may also be allowed to fancy that the first sensations were purely direct, that is to say that man saw without precision, heard confusedly, smelt without discernment, eat without savour, and was in fact little better than a brute in all his enjoyments.

But as all these sensations have the soul as a common centre–the especial distinction of the human species–and the ever active cause of a striving towards perfection, they became modified, swayed by judgment and comparison, and soon all the senses came to the aid of each other for the benefit of the sensitive being or individual.

Thus the sense of touch rectified the errors of sight; sound, by means of articulated words, became the interpreter of every sentiment; taste became benefited by sight and smell; hearing compared sounds and appreciated distances.

The torrent of centuries rolling over the human race has incessantly engendered new perfections, the cause of which, though almost invisible, is to be found in the play of the senses, which, in rotation, exact agreeable employment.

Thus sight gave rise to painting, sculpture, and all sorts of displays.

Sound gave birth to melody, to harmony, to dance, and music, and all their branches.

Smell to the discovery and cultivation of perfumes.

Taste to the production, selection, and preparation of every species of food.

Touch gave birth to every branch of industry.

A man who has dined at a sumptuous table, in a hall resplendent with mirrors, pictures, statuary, flowers, delicate perfumes, adorned with beautiful women, and enlivened by the sound of soft music will not need much mental effort to be convinced that all the sciences have been placed under contribution to heighten and crown the enjoyments of taste.

Taste is that one of our senses which brings us in contact with sapid substances, through the medium of the sensation they produce upon the organ destined to appreciate them.

Taste is aroused by appetite, hunger, and thirst; it is the basis of many operations, the result of which is that the individual grows, developes, lives, and repairs the losses caused by vital evaporations.

All organised bodies are not nourished in the same manner; the author of creation, as diverse in his methods as he is sure in their effect, has assigned to them various means of conservation.

Vegetables, which must be placed at the bottom of the scale of living things, draw their nourishment through roots which, implanted in the soil, select, by the action of a peculiar mechanism, the various substances which are proper for their growth and preservation.

If we go a step higher we find bodies possessing animal life but deprived of locomotion; they are born in a centre which favours their existence; and especial organs enable them to extract from around them whatever is necessary to sustain that length and portion of vitality granted to them; they do not seek their food, their food comes to them.

Another method was ordained for the preservation of the animals of the earth, of which man is incontestably the most perfect. A peculiar instinct advises him to get food; he looks around him, he seizes upon the objects in which he fancies there is property to satisfy his wants; he eats, feels restored, and thus fulfils the career pointed out for him.

Taste appears to have two principal functions:– 1. It invites us by pleasure to repair the continual losses we incur by the action of life.

2. It aids us to select amongst the various substances which nature offers us those most suitable for food.

In this selection, taste is powerfully aided by smell, as we shall see further on; for it may be asserted as a general maxim that nutritious substances are not repulsive either to taste or smell.

The number of flavours is infinite, for every substance capable of solution has a peculiar flavour of its own.

The sense of smell has a great influence on taste. I am inclined to believe that taste and smell are one and the same sense, the laboratory of which is the mouth, and the nose the chimney. The nose is a sentinel, and is always on the alert to cry, Whos there?

Take away the sense of smell, and that of taste goes with it.

This principle once put, I maintain that there are three distinct orders of taste, viz. direct sensation; complete sensation; and the sensation of judgment.

Direct sensation is the first impression from the contact of the food with the organs of the mouth whilst on the point of the tongue.

Complete sensation consists of the first sensation and the impression arising from it when the morsel of food leaves the first position, passes to the back of the mouth, and strikes the whole organ with its taste and perfume.

Finally, the sensation of judgment is that of the mind, which reflects upon the impression transmitted by the organ.

Let us have an example:—

The man who eats a peach is first agreeably struck by its fragrance; he puts a slice in his mouth, and experiences a sensation of freshness and acidity, which induces him to continue; but it is only at the moment he swallows that the real perfume of the peach is revealed; this is the complete sensation caused by a peach.

Finally, it is only when he has swallowed the morsel that he can exclaim: " That was delicious!"

The same may be said of a man who drinks a good glass of wine. As long as the wine is in his mouth he experiences an agreeable, but not a perfect impression. It is only when he has swallowed the liquid that he really can taste, appreciate, and discern the particular perfume of the wine; and then a few minutes must be allowed to the gourmet to give vent to his feelings, by: " Peste, dest du Chambertin /" or, " Mon Dieu! cest du Sursne!"

This will suffice to prove that your real connois seur sips his wine; at every sip he takes he has the sum total of the pleasure which another man enjoys when he swallows a whole glass.

Let us take an opposite example.

A doctor orders a man to take a black draught.

His nose, a faithful sentinel, warns him of the treacherous liquor he is about to imbibe. His eyes become globular, as at the approach of danger; disgust is on his lips; his stomach rises. He is encouraged by the doctor, he gargles his throat with brandy, pinches his nose, and drinks.

As long as the detestable beverage fills his mouth, the sensation is confused and supportable; but when the last drop disappears the sickening flavours act, and the patient makes a grimace which the fear of death alone would warrant.

If it is a glass of water, there is no taste; he drinks, swallows, and that is all.

Taste is not so richly endowed as hearing; the latter sense can compare divers sounds at the same time; taste, on the contrary is simple in actuality, that is to say, it cannot be impressioned by two flavours at the same time.

But it may be double and even multiplied by succession; that is to say, in the same act of gut-turation, a second and even a third sensation may be experienced, which gradually lessens, and which is designated aandarriandre-gout, perfume or fragrance; in the same manner as, when a keynote is struck, a practised ear discerns one or more sonances, the number of which has not yet been accurately ascertained. f

Hasty and careless eaters do not discern the impression in the second degree; they are the exclusive property of a small body of elect; and it is by their means that they can classify, in order of excellence, the various substances submitted to their examination.

These fugitive nuances of flavour remain for some time on the palate; the professors assume, without being aware of it, an appropriate position, and it is always with an elongated neck and a twist of the nose that they pronounce their judgment.

Let us now take a philosophical glance at the pleasure or unpleasantness taste may occasion.

We first find the application of that, unhappily, too general. truth, that man is more organised for suffering than for experiencing pleasure.

In fact, the injection of very bitter, acid, or tart substances may cause us the sensation of excruciating pain. It is even supposed that hydrocyanic acid only kills so rapidly because it causes such excruciating agony that the vital powers cannot support it.

Agreeable sensations, on the contrary, are on a limited scale, and though there is a marked difference between what is insipid and what is palatable, there is no great interval between what is admitted to be good and what is reputed excellent; for example, 1st term, hard boiled beef; 2nd term, a piece of veal; 3rd term, a pheasant roasted to a turn.

Yet taste, such as nature has awarded it to us, is still that sense which, well considered, procures us the greatest degree of enjoyment.

1st. Because the pleasure of eating is the only one which, done in moderation, is not followed by fatigue.

2nd. Because it is of all times, all ages, all conditions.

3rd. Because it returns necessarily, at least once a day, and may be repeated, without inconvenience, two or three times within the same period of time.

4th. Because it may be enjoyed with other enjoyments, and even console us for their absence.

5th. Because its impressions are more durable more dependent on our will, and 6th, and finally. Because in eating we experience a certain indescribable sensation of pleasure, which emanates from instinctive consciousness; by what we eat we repair the losses we have sustained, and prolong life.

This subject is more amply developed in Chapter XII., in which we discuss "the pleasures of the table," in the point of view of the present state of civilisation.

We were brought up in the flattering belief that of all creatures that walk, swim, crawl, or fly, man was the one whose taste was most perfect.

This faith is threatened with being upset.

Dr. Gail, on what grounds I know not, pretends that there are animals whose organ of taste is much more developed and perfect than is that of man.

Such doctrine smacks of heresy.

Man, by divine right, king of all he surveys, for whose benefit the earth was covered and peopled, must necessarily be provided with an organ to place him in contact with all that is sapid amongst his subjects.

The tongue of animals is in proportion to their intelligence; in fishes it is simply a moveable bone; in birds, generally speaking, a membraneous cartilage; in quadrupeds it is often covered with scales or points, and moreover has no circumflex movement.

The tongue of man, on the contrary, by the delicacy of its conformation and of the diverse membranes by which it is surrounded or which are close to it, announces plain enough the sublimity of the operations to which it is destined.

I have, moreover, discovered at least three movements unknown to animals, and which I call movements of spication, rotation, and verrition

The first takes place when the tongue leaves the lips which compress it; the second when the tongue makes a circular movement round the space comprised between the interior of the cheeks and the palate; the third when the tongue, turning over or under, picks up the atoms which may remain in the semicircular canal formed by the lips and gums.

Animals are limited in their tastes; some live exclusively upon vegetables; others only eat flesh; others feed upon grain; not one understands a combined flavour.

Man, on the contrary, is omnivorous; every thing eatable becomes a prey to his vast appetite; which at once implies digestive powers proportionate to the general use he puts them to. In fact, the machinery of taste in man is of rare perfection, and to be convinced of the fact let us see it act.

From the Latin verb verro, I sweep.

As soon as an esculent substance is introduced into the mouth it is confiscated, gas and juices, irretrievably.

The lips prevent its leaving; the teeth seize upon it and crush it; the saliva absorbs it; the tongue bruises it and turns it round; the breath forces it towards the gullet; the tongue again rises to make it slip down; the sense of smell enjoys it as it glides past, and it is precipitated into the stomach to undergo ulterior transformations, without, during the whole of this operation, the slightest atom, particle, or drop being lost, which has not been submitted to the appreciating power.

And a consequence of this perfection is that gourmandise is the exclusive apanage of man.

This gourmandise is even contagious; and we transmit it promptly to the animals we have in our service, and which become, in a certain measure, our companions, as elephants, dogs, cats, and even parrots.

If some animals have a larger tongue than others, a more developed palate, a wider swallow, it is because that tongue, as a muscle, is meant to move heavier morsels, to press and swallow larger portions; but no logic can prove that the sense of taste is more perfect.

Moreover, as taste can only be esteemed by the nature of the sensation it procures to the common centre, the impression received by an animal cannot be compared to that received by a man; the latter impression, being more clear and more precise, naturally, implies a superior quality in the organ which transmits it.

Finally, what greater refinement of taste can be desired, when a Eoman bon-vivant could at once tell whether a fish had been caught above or below bridge? And in our own days, a real good eater discovers at once the superior flavour of the leg of the partridge upon which it has slept. And do we not know gourmets who can tell in what latitude a grape has ripened, from the wine I they sip, with as much preciseness as Arago would predict an eclipse?

. And what results herefrom? Let us render to Caesar that which is Caesars, proclaim man the great gourmand of nature, and not be astonished if Gall, like Homer, sometimes "sleeps."

Hitherto we have examined taste only in the light of its physical constitution, and we have kept to the level of science. But our task does not end here, for it is especially in the moral history of this repairing sense that its importance and its glory ought to be sought.

We have therefore arranged, according to analytical order, the theories and facts which constitute this history, that instruction may result without fatigue. Thus in the chapters which follow, we shall endeavour to show how sensations from repetition and reflection have perfected the organ, and extended the sphere of its powers; how the want of eating, at first only an instinct, became a passion of influence which has assumed a marked ascendency over everything else connected with society.

We will also point out how all branches of science, which have reference to the composition of substances, act in concert to place apart those which are appreciable to taste, and how travellers have worked towards the same end by submitting to our examination substances which nature seemingly never meant to bring together.

We will follow chemistry from the moment it entered our subterraneous laboratories to enlighten our cooks, lay down principles, create methods and reveal causes which have hitherto remained secret.

Finally, we shall see how, by the combined power of time and experience, a new science arose, which nourishes, restores, preserves, persuades, consoles, and, not satisfied with strewing flowers by handfuls along the path of man, contributes also powerfully to the strength and prosperity of empires.

If in the midst of these grave lucubrations a piquant anecdote, an amiable souvenir, some adventure of an agitated career, should drop from our pen, let it pass, to give a rest to our readers attention, whose number does not alarm us, and with whom we are always glad to chat; for if they are men, we feel convinced they are as indulgent as they are well informed; if they are ladies, they cannot be otherwise than charming.

Here the professor, replete with his subject, let his pen drop and soared in high regions. Mentally he passes through the course of the torrents of ages, visits in their cradle those sciences whose object is the gratification of taste. He fol lowed their progress through the night of time, and beholding that the enjoyments which they procure for us were less advantageous in the earlier centuries than those which followed, he seized his lyre, and in the Dorian style he sang, in inspired tones, the following historical elegy:

"Ye first parents of the human race, whose gourmandise is the province of history, who lost yourselves for an apple, what would you not have done for a turkey stuffed with truffles? But in the terrestrial paradise there were neither cooks nor confectioners.

Oh! how I pity you!

"Ye powerful kings who ruined superb Troy, the memory of your valour will descend to all ages; but you fared badly. Eestricted to the thigh of an ox, or a pigs back, you were ignorant of the delights of a matelote, and the savours of a fricasseed chicken.

Oh! how I pity you!

"Aspasia, Chloe, and all ye whose forms have been immortalised by the chisel of the Greeks to the great despair of our modern belles, never did your charming lips taste the delicate flavour of a meringue a la vanille, or a Ja rose; you scarcely rose to the dignity of ginger-bread.

Oh! how I pity you!

"Gentle priestesses of Vesta, upon whom so many honours as well as terrible menaces of horrible tortures were showered at the same time, if at least you had moistened your lips with those amiable simps which gladden the soul, those preserved fruits which defy the seasons, those perfumed creams, the wonders of modern times!

Oh! how I pity you!

"Ye Roman financiers, who extorted from the whole known universe, never did your famed salons behold those succulent. jellies, nor those varied ices, the cold of which equals that of the arctic zone.

Oh! how I pity you!

"Invincible paladins, celebrated by troubadours, after slaying giants, delivering fair damsels, exterminating armies, never, alas! never did a black-eyed captive present you with a bottle of Champagne mousseux, Malvoisie, or Madeira, or liqueurs, creations of the great century. You were reduced to cherry-brandy, or a cider-cup.

Oh! how I pity you I

"Ye croziercd and mitred abbots, dispensers of the favours of Heaven; and ye terrible Templars, who donned armour for the extermination of the Saracen, you knew not of the restoring powers of chocolate, or of the Arabian berry which engenders dreams.

Oh! how I pity you!

"Ye superb mother abbesses, who, during the void caused by the Crusades, elevated to supreme rank your almoners and your pages, you did not share with them the charms of biscuits, nor the delight of macaroons.

Oh! how I pity you!

"And you, finally, gastronomers of 1825, who find already satiety in the midst of abundance and dream of new concoctions, ye will not be able to enjoy the discoveries which science is preparing for the year 1900, such as the extractions from minerals, liqueurs resulting from the pressure of a hundred atmospheres; you will never behold the importations which still unborn future travellers will bring home from that portion of the globe still to be discovered or explored.

Oh! how I pity you!"

CHAP. V.

GASTRONOMY.–ORIGIN OF THE SCIENCES.

The sciences do not resemble Minerva, who issued forth armed cap-a-pie from the brain of Jupiter; they are the daughters of time, are formed invisibly, first by the collection of methods indicated by experience, and later by the discovery of principles deducted from the combination of those methods.

Thus the first old men whose prudence made the invalid send for them, whose compassion induced them to bandage wounds, were also the first physicians.

The shepherds of Egypt, who observed that certain planets after a certain lapse of time reappeared on the same line of the horizon, were the first astronomers.

The man who first expressed in characters that very simple proposition "twice two make four " created mathematics that powerful science which has in reality placed man on the throne of the universe.

In the course of the last sixty years, various new sciences have taken a place in the system of our knowledge, as stereotomy, descriptive geometry, electricity, and the chemistry of gas.

All these sciences, cultivated for an infinity of generations, will make still more certain progress, since the art of printing will prevent them from being lost. And who knows, for instance, whether the chemistry of gas may not some day succeed in dompting those elements hitherto eo rebellious, of mixing them, combining them in proportions hitherto unattempted, of obtaining by such means substances and effects which would extend beyond measure the limits of our powers?

Gastronomy presented herself in her turn, and all her sisters received her with open arms.

And what could be refused to a science which nourishes us from our birth until our death; which increases the enjoyments of love, the pleasures of friendship; which disarms hatred, facilitates business, and offers us in the short passage of life the only enjoyment which, not being followed by fatigue, relieves us from all others?

Doubtless when everything was trusted to the hands of an ordinary cook it remained in an imperfect state. But men of science finally took it up. They examined, analysed, and classified, the different alimentary substances, and reduced them to their simple elements.

They fathomed the mysteries of assimilation; and following inert matter through all its changes, they discovered how to give it life. They watched a diet in its passing or permanent effects, daily, monthly, for a whole life. They investigated its influence even on the mind, as regards the effect produced upon it by the senses as well as its powers when the senses are dormant; and from all those labours they deducted a grand theory which embraces the whole of mankind and every portion of creation capable of animal life.

Whilst these things were taking place in the cabinets of scientific men, in the dining-hall it was loudly maintained that the science which nourished man was at least as valuable as that which taught how to kill him; poets sang the pleasures of the table, and works on good cheer became more instructive and important.

These were the circumstances which preceded the advent of gastronomy.

Gastronomy is the maturer knowledge–the rationale of everything which concerns man-as regards his food.

Its object is the preservation of man by providing him with the best possible food.

It succeeds in doing so by guiding, by certain principles, all those who seek, provide, or prepare food.

In fact, it may be said that it is the motor of the agriculturist, the vine-grower, the sportsman, the fisherman, and the great family of cooks, under whatever name they may disguise their occupation in the preparation or procurance of articles of food.

Gastronomy is connected:–

With natural history by the classification it makes of alimentary substances;

With physics by the examination of their composition and quality;

With chemistry by the different analyses and decompositions it subjects them to;

With cookery by the art of preparing the dishes and making them agreeable to the taste;

With commerce by seeking the cheapest and best market to buy in, and an advantageous one to sell in;

Finally, with political economy by the returns it brings into the Exchequer, and the means of exchange it provides to nations.

Gastronomy rules the whole life of man; the first cries of the new-born babe are for its nurses breast; and a man on his death-bed swallows still with some pleasure the last potion, which, alas! he has not the power to digest.

Moreover, it is closely linked with every class of society: it presides at the banquet of a congress of kings, and also is present to calculate how many minutes are necessary to boil an egg to the proper turn.

The material subject of gastronomy is everything that can be eaten; its direct object the. preservation of the individual; its means of execution, cultivation which produces, commerce which exchanges, industry which prepares, and experience which invents the means to turn everything to the best account.

Gastronomy considers taste in its enjoyments as well as in its drawbacks; it has discovered the various degrees of pleasure it produces; it has regulated their action, and has fixed limits which no man of self-respect ought to outstep.

It considers also the action of food on the moral qiialities of man, on his imagination, his mind, his judgment, his courage and perceptions, whether awake or asleep, whether moving or reposing.

It is gastronomy, again, which fixes the exact point when an article of food ought to be used, for all are not presentable under the same circumstances.

Some ought to be used before they have attained their full development, as capers, asparagus, sucking-pigs, pigeons, andc.; others, when they have attained full maturity, as melons, most fruits, mutton, beef, and all adult animals; others, when decomposition commences, as medlars, woodcocks and especially the pheasant; others, again, when their disagreeable qualities have been removed, as the potato, tapioca and others.

It is gastronomy, again, which classifies these substances according to their various qualities, and gives them their proper place at the dining-table. It devotes no less interest to beverages, classifying them according to date of vintage, clime, and locality. It teaches how to prepare and preserve them, but especially how to present them in an order so exactly calculated, that the enjoyment resulting therefrom always increases until pleasure ceases and abuse commences.

It is gastronomy which passes in review men and things, that it may convey from one country to another what is worthy of being known, and which makes a well-organised banquet an abrege of the world, where each part has its representative.

The knowledge of gastronomy is necessary to-all men, because it increases the amount of pleasure allotted to them. This increases in proportion to the wealth of society; it becomes indispensable to men who have large fortunes, give grand dinners, and sail in the wake of fashion.

They find this special advantage therein, that, on their part, there is something personal in the manner in which their table is served; they take an interest, can superintend, and, to a certain degree, direct the men in whom they must necessarily place confidence.

The Prince de Soubise had, one day, the intention of giving a fete; it was to terminate with a supper, and he asked to see his bill of fare.

His maitre-dhotel waited upon him at his levee with the required document. The very first item which caught the Princes eye was fifty hams!

"What! Bertrand," he exclaimed, "I think you are extravagant: fifty hams! Do you wish to sup my whole regiment?" "No, my Prince, only one ham will appear at supper; but the remainder are indispensable to me for my espagnole, my blonds, my trimmings, my." "Bertrand, you are robbing me, and I will not allow that item." "Ah, Monseigneur," said the artiste, scarcely able to suppress his anger, "you do not know our capabilities! Say the word, and those fifty hams, which annoy you, I will put them all in a crystal flacon not bigger than the top of my thumb."

Cotelettes a la Soubise are still a famous dish: a white sauce with the echo of onions. Very well cooked at the Garrick.

What reply could be made to so positive an assertion? The Prince smiled, nodded his head, and the item passed.

It is a matter of history, that, amongst tribes which are still of a primitive nature, no affair of importance is concluded without a feast; it is at banquets that savages decide upon war or make peace; and, without going further, all villagers conclude their bargains at the pot-house.

This did not escape the observation of those who have often to treat the most important affairs of state; they saw that your well-filled man was a different being than when fasting; that the dinner-table formed a sort of link between the host and the guest; that the latter was more open to receive impressions it was desirable to make, more ready to submit to certain influences. This gave rise to political gastronomy; dinners became a means of government, arid the fate of nations is often decided at a dinner. This is neither paradox nor novel, but a simple matter of every-day observation. Open any historian, from Herodotus down to the present day, and, not even excepting conspiracies, it may be said, that no great event ever occurred without having been conceived, prepared, and determined upon at a feast.

Such is the superficial glance at the domain of gastronomy, a domain fertile in results of every description, and which cannot but advance with the onward march of science; for in a few years gastronomy must have its academy, its lectures, its professors, its prizes.

First, some rich and zealous gastronome will invite his friends to his table at fixed periods to discuss, in conjunction with learned theoricians and artistes, some interesting point of alimentary science. Soon (and this is the history of all academies) government will intervene, regulate, protect, institute. Thrice happy the man whose name will figure as the founder of such an academy. His name will be handed down to all posterity with the names of Noah, Bacchus, Triptolemus and other benefactors of man; he will be amongst ministers what Henry IV. is amongst kings, and his praise will be in every mans mouth without any law to compel it.

CHAP. VI.

ON APPETITE.

Movement and life occasion in a living body a continual loss of substance; and the human body, that complicated machine, would soon be out of order if Providence had not given it a sentinel to warn it of the moment that its powers were no longer in equal balance with its wants.

That sentinel is appetite. The word implies the first impression of the desire to eat.

Appetite announces itself by a feeling of languor in the stomach and a slight sensation of fatigue. At the same time the mind becomes occupied with subjects analogous to its wants; memory recalls things which have pleased the taste; imagination brings them up vividly; it becomes a sort of dream. This state is not devoid of a certain charm, and we have heard many adepts exclaim, in the gladness of their hearts, "What a pleasure it is to have a good appetite, when one is certain of soon having an excellent dinner!

Nevertheless the whole system gradually becomes aroused: the stomach becomes growly; the gastric juices increase; the gases inside become active; the mouth fills with juices, and all the digestive powers are up in arms like soldiers, only awaiting the word of command to charge. A little longer and spasms would succeed, yawning,–in short, hunger.

All these various shades may be observed in a drawing-room, where men are waiting for dinner.

They are so inherent in mans nature that the most refined politeness cannot subdue the symptoms. Whence I maintain as a maxim:–" Punctuality is The Most Indispensable Quality In A Cook."

I will support this grave maxim by relating a little experience I had myself at a dinner to which I was invited–

"Quorum pars magna fui,"

and where the pleasure of observation saved me from the pangs of misery.

I was invited one day to dine with a great public functionary. The hour mentioned was half-past five, and punctually to the minute all the guests had arrived; they all knew the hosts punctuality, and that he always plucked a crow with late comers.

I arrived a minute or so late, and was struck on entering at a certain appearance of consternation on the countenances of the guests. There were whisperings going on; some were staring through the window panes into the court-yard; some faces betrayed annoyance; it was quite clear something unusual had occurred. I approached one of the guests whom I thought likely to enlighten me, and asked him what had happened.

"Alas!" he said, in a voice of deep affliction, "Monseigneur has just been summoned to a state cabinet-council: he is just going, and God knows when he will be back!"

"Is that all? " I said, with a nonchalance which was far from real. " It is a little matter, which will be over in a quarter of an hour–some point they wish to be informed upon; they are aware he has an official dinner to-day, they will not keep us fasting." I spoke thus, but my heart sank within me, and I wished myself far away.

The first hour passed pretty well: men who knew each other sat down and chatted, the usual light topics of the day were discussed, and conjectures were made why our Amphitryon had been so suddenly called to the Tuileries.

As the clock struck the second hour, some signs of impatience were evinced; men looked at each other with an anxious expression of countenance, and faint murmurs came from the lips of two or three who not having found places to sit, were tired of waiting and standing.

At the third hour discontent became general, and every one gave vent to his plaints. " When will he come back? " said one; "What the d–l is he doing!" exclaims another; "It is abominable!" shouts a third; and the question was raised more than once whether it would not be better to go.

At the fourth the symptoms became aggravated; some stretched their arms, at the risk of putting out an eye of a neighbour; yawns echoed through the apartment; some faces began to assume a livid look, and when I hazarded the observation that he whose absence made us all so sad was most probably the most annoyed of us all, a deaf ear was turned to me.

Attention was for a moment aroused by one of the guests. Being on more intimate terms than the others, he had made a descent into the kitchens; he came back out of breath; he looked as if about to announce the end of the world, and. exclaimed in a broken voice, subdued yet anxious to make itself heard, "Monseigneur left no orders, and no matter how long he stays away, dinner cannot be served till his return." He ceased, and his speech created an effect not easily described.

Of all these martyrs, poor kind-hearted daigre-feuille was the most unhappy; his whole frame denoted suffering, and the anguish oflaocoon was on his face. Pale, wild-looking, almost blind, he let himself drop upon a sofa, crossed his. fat little hands over his paunch, and shut his eyes, riot to go to sleep, but to await death. It however did not come. About ten oclock a carriage rolled into the court-yard; all rose by a spontaneous movement. Hilarity succeeded discontent, and in five minutes all were at table.

But the hour of appetite had passed. They seemed surprised they should commence dinner at so unusual an hour; the jaws did not display that isochrone movement which announces good work; and I learnt afterwards that some of the guests were ill after it.

In cases like the above the method to be adopted is this; not to commence eating at once, but first swallow a glass of eau sucree or a cup of bouillon to console the stomach, and then wait ten or fifteen minutes, otherwise the organ which has got out of order feels oppressed by the weight of food forced upon it.

When we see in books of an early period the preparations which were made to dine two or three persons, and the enormous quantity served to. one guest, we can scarcely help believing that men of past ages had greater appetites than ourselves.

That appetite was greater according to the rank of the personage was a common notion, and the dignitary who had half a five-year-old ox served before him was doomed to quaff from a goblet he could scarcely lift.

Some individuals have been found in modern times who bear witness to the feats of the past; and there are examples of voracious appetites on record scarcely credible. I will spare my readers these often disgusting details, but will give two facts which I myself witnessed.

Some forty years since I paid a flying visit to the Cure of Bregnier, a man of large stature, and noted for his appetite. Though scarcely noon, I found him already at table. The soup and bouilli had been removed, and a gigot of mutton a la royale, a fine capon, and large bowl of salad were brought in.

He politely offered me a knife and fork which I declined, and it was well I did so, for fie very soon polished off everything, eating the mutton till nothing was left but the bone, picking the capon till it was a mere skeleton, and emptying the bowl of salad. A huge cheese was then put on the table, in which the worthy cure made an angular breach of ninety-nine degrees. He washed down the whole with a bottle of wine and a decanter of water, after which he reposed.

What pleased me was to observe that during the whole of this performance, which took about three quarters of an hour, the venerable pastor did not display the slightest hurry. The huge morsels he threw into his capacious mouth did not prevent him from chatting and laughing, and he finished everything with as much ease as if he had only eaten three larks.

In like manner, General Bisson, who drank eight bottles of wine every morning at breakfast, did not betray it; his glass was larger than the others, and he emptied it oftener; but all this so quietly, that a stranger would not have supposed he had drunk more than a bottle.

The second case brings back to my memory my brave compatriot General P. Sibuet, for a long time first aide-de-camp of General Massena, and killed at the passage of the Bober, in 1813.

Prosper, at the age of eighteen, was a fine young man, with that happy appetite which promised well for further development. He one afternoon entered the kitchen of Genin, where the " ancients " of Belley used to meet to discuss chestnuts and a white wine called win bourru.

A magnificent turkey had just been taken off the spit, well-shaped, golden, done to a turn, and the odour from which was enough to tempt a saint.

The "ancients," most of whom had dined, did not pay much attention to the savoury bird, but the digestive powers of young Prosper were stirred within him; his mouth watered, and he exclaimed, "I have only just dined, but I will lay a wager I will eat the whole of that turkey myself." " Sez vosu meze, z u payo," responded Bouvier du Bouchet, a stalwart farmer who was present, " e sez vos caca en rotaz, i-zet vo ket paire et may ket mezerai la restaz."

The young athlete set to work at once. He cut off a wing which he swallowed in two morsels; after which he cleaned his teeth by crunching the neck of the bird, and swallowed a glass of wine as an entr acte.

If you will eat it, I will pay for it; bat if you break down, you will pay for it, and I eat the rest.

He then attacked a thigh, ate it with the same sangfroid, and took another glass of wine to prepare the way for the remainder. The second wing soon followed the first, and with increased zest he was about to dispatch the remaining limb, when the unfortunate farmer, with a doleful voice, stopped him, exclaiming, "Hai l ze vraie praou qui-zet fota; mez, monche Chibouet, poez kaet za daive, lesse men a m en mesiet on mocho."

Prosper was as good a fellow as he was a good soldier; he consented, and the farmer got the carcass, no bad part, and cheerfully paid the bill for the turkey and accessories.

General Sibuet used often to relate with pleasure this feat of his youth, always maintaining that it was simply from courtesy that he allowed tjie farmer a morsel, and that he would have won the wager with ease, fully confident of his powers, and those who knew his appetite when he was forty had no need to doubt the assertion.

Alas! I see it is dtine; but, M. Sibuet, as I have to pay for it, let me at least eat a little bit myself.

CHAP. VII.

ON FOOD.

What is food? The general definition is: Everything which nourishes us. The scientific definition is this: By food we mean those substances which, submitted to the stomach, are susceptible of ani-malisation by means of digestion, and repair the losses which the human body suffers from the course of life.

Thus, the distinctive quality of food consists in the property of undergoing animal assimilation.

The animal kingdom and the vegetable kingdom are those which have hitherto provided food to the human species. As yet, nothing has been extracted from minerals but remedies or poisons.

Since analytic chemistry has become an adopted science, great steps in advance have been made in ascertaining the double nature of the elements of which the human body consists, and in discovering the substances which nature seems to have destined to restore the losses it sustains,

There is great analogy between these studies, as man consists in a great measure of the same substances as the animals upon which he feeds, and it became necessary to endeavour to discover in vegetables those affinities in consequence of which they also became susceptible of animali-sation.

In these two branches the most praiseworthy, and at the same time most minute investigations have been undertaken, and an analysis has been made as well of the human body as of the food which sustains it, first in their secondary departments and then in their elements, beyond which there is a veil which we have not been allowed to penetrate.

The greatest service rendered by chemistry to alimentary science is the discovery, or rather the precise knowledge obtained, of "osmazome." Osmazome is that eminently sapid portion of meat which is soluble in cold water, and which differs from that extractive portion which is only soluble in boiling water.

The merit of a good soup or broth consists in osmazome. It forms the brown (rissole) on roasts, the rich gravy; it gives the flavour to venison and other game.

It is to be found chiefly in full-grown animals, and rarely in white meat, as veal, sucking-pigs, or capons. Your real connoisseur always prefers the inner thigh of a fowl, the instinct of taste having anticipated science.

The discovery of the qualities of osmazome has led to the dismissal of many cooks convicted of extracting the first soup or bouillon; it formed the groundwork of all great soups; it introduced a cup of broth as a beverage after a bath, and induced the Abbe Chevrier to invent cauldrons with lock and key. It is this same abbe who, when he had spinach on the Friday, had it cooked on the Sunday before, and replaced on the fire every day, with an addition of fresh butter, until served up.

Finally, to understand the management of this substance (in other words, to make good broth), you must never allow it to more than smile (simmer),–not a bad expression, considering whence it came.

The qualities of osmazome, discovered after having for centuries been the delight of our forefathers, may be compared to those of alcohol, which had inebriated many generations before it
was discovered that it might be extracted pure by distillation.

After the osmazome, by the power of boiling water is produced what is generally termed extractive matter; this latter production, mixed up with the osmazome, forms the juice of beef.

To carve well, always cut at a right angle with the fibres of your joint; a joint well carved is more agreeable to the eye, pleasanter to the taste, and is more easily chewed.

HOW TO MAKE SOUP OR BHOTH.

To make a good soup or broth, your water must be allowed to boil gradually, to prevent the albumen from coagulating before it is extracted; the boiling must be scarcely evident, so that all the component parts may dissolve and mix gradually and quietly. A few vegetables or roots may be added to give a flavour, or bread or paste (macaroni) to give more nourishment.

This is a very wholesome food, being light, nutritious and suitable to all. It gives tone to the digestive organs. Men inclined to grow corpulent should take nothing but soup.

You rarely get a better soup than you do in France.

POULTRY.

The whole race of fowls was created to furnish our larders and adorn our banquets.

From the quail to the turkey, wherever we stumble upon a member of that numerous family, we are sure to find a light, savoury dish, suitable to the invalid as well as to the man in the most robust health.

Where is the man who has been sentenced by his doctor to the food of the pilgrim in the desert, whose lips will not play with a joyous smile when a neatly cut wing of chicken is placed before him? It announces to him that he has been restored to social life.

We are not satisfied with the qualities nature has given to the gallinaceous breed. Art stepped in, and, under the mask of improvement, made martyrs. They are isolated, stuffed, and brought to a size which they never were meant to attain.

It is true that this extra fat is very delicious, and that it is by these damnable means that they acquire that succulence and delicacy which form the delights of our best dinners.

Thus improved, poultry is to the kitchen what canvas is to the artist.

We have it served up boiled, fried, roasted, hot, cold, whole, hashed, with or without sauce, boned, grilled, stuffed, and always eat it with pleasure.

THE TURKEY.

The turkey is assuredly one of the noblest gifts the New World has given to the Old.

Men who pretend to be wiser than their betters have asserted that the turkey was known to the Romans, that it was served up at the marriage of Charlemagne, and that it is an error to attribute to the Jesuits the honour of this savoury importation.

To that paradox two objections would suffice:– 1. The name of the bird, which attests its origin: for formerly America was designated by the name of Indes Occidentales; hence dindon.

2. The appearance of the bird, which is evidently foreign.

Nevertheless, though perfectly convinced I was right, I made very extended researches on the subject, the result of which was: 1. That the turkey was introduced into Europe towards the end of the seventeenth century.

2. That it was introduced by the Jesuits, who bred a large number, chiefly at a farm which they possessed near Bourges.

3. That it was from thence they gradually spread over France; and still in many parts of France jesuite is a familiar term for turkey.

4. That America is the only locality where the wild turkey has been found in a state of nature. There are not any in Africa.

5. That in the farms of North America, where it is very common, it is reared either from eggs which have been taken, or from wild turkeys that have been caught young and tamed; this makes them retain more closely their primitive plumage.

Convinced by these proofs, I owe a second expression of gratitude to the worthy fathers for having introduced quinine, which is still known as Jesuits bark.

The same researches proved to me that the turkey gradually becomes acclimatised in Europe. About the middle of last century scarcely ten out of twenty young birds thrived, whilst now the proportions are at least fifteen. Heavy rain especially is fatal to them. Heavy drops of rain driven by the wind, falling upon their tender and uncovered head, speedily kills them.

The turkey is the largest, and if not the most delicate is at least the most savoury of our domestic fowls.

It also has the exclusive advantage of assembling around it all classes of society.

When our vine-growers and farmers give a feast on a long winters night, what do we behold turning on the spit before a hot fire in the kitchen where the cloth is laid?–a turkey.

When the useful manufacturer, the hard-working artisan, wishes to give a treat to his friends, the obligato dish is a turkey stuffed with chestnuts and sausages.

And in our high gastronomic circles, in those select reunions where politics are obliged to give way to a dissertation on taste,–what is expected? what is brought up at the second course?–a truffled turkey! And my private memoranda contain a note that its restoring juices have more than once enlightened countenances eminently diplomatic.

The importation of turkeys has become the cause of an important addition to the public purse, and has given rise to a considerable trade. By the rearing of turkeys the farmers are enabled to be more ready to pay their rent and give their daughters marriage portions; and the good citizens who wish to regale on such delicacies must open their purse-strings wide. In this financial point of view, truffled turkeys deserve particular mention. I have reason to believe that from the commencement of November to the end of February 300 truffled turkeys are consumed daily in Paris, altogether 36,000 turkeys. The usual price of each is, at least, 20 francs, in all 720,000 francs, no small circulation of specie. To this must be added a similar sum for fowls, pheasants, chickens, and partridges, also truffled, which may be seen daily displayed in the windows of eating-houses, to the torture of the passers by who cannot afford to purchase them.

During my sojourn at Hartford, in Connecticut, I had the happiness to shoot a wild turkey. That exploit deserves to be handed down to posterity, and I will relate it the more readily as I myself am the hero.

An old American farmer invited me to pay him a visit for shooting; he lived in the back-woods; he promised me grey squirrels, partridges, wild-cocks (wild turkeys), and told me to bring one or two friends of my own choice with me.

One fine day in October, 1794, a friend of mine, Mr. King, and myself, mounted on hacks, set out in the hope of reaching, towards evening, Mr. Bulows farm, distant five mortal leagues from Hartford, Connecticut.

Mr. King was a peculiar sort of sportsman; he was passionately fond of the exercise, but as soon as he had brought down his bird he looked upon himself as a murderer, and made moral reflections and elegies over the game, which, however, did not prevent him from recommencing.

Although the path was scarcely traced, we arrived without accident, and were received with that cordial and quiet hospitality which is expressed by acts; that is to say, in a few moments everything was examined, caressed, and lodged, man, horse, and dogs, according to custom.

Two hours were devoted to visit the farm and its dependencies; I might give a description of it, but prefer presenting the reader to four buxom lasses, Mr. Bulows daughters, and for whom our arrival was a great event.

Their ages varied from sixteen to twenty; they were radiant with freshness and health; and there was so much simplicity in all their movements, so much natural grace, that the most ordinary action sufficed to give them a thousand charms.

Shortly after our promenade, we sat down round a well-provided table. A magnificent piece of corned beef, a stewed goose, and a splendid haunch of mutton, vegetables in plenty, and two huge foaming pots of excellent cider.

When we had proved to our host that we were good sportsmen, at least as far as appetite went, he entered into the object of our visit. He indicated the best places where we were likely to find game, the landmarks to observe to guide us back, and especially the farm-houses where we could get refreshment.

Whilst we were thus conversing, the ladies were preparing tea, so excellent that we drank two or three cups of it; after which we were shown into a double-bedded room, where exercise and good cheer soon sent us into a profound sleep.

On the morrow we started somewhat late on our expedition, and having reached the limits of Mr. Bulows clearings, I found myself for the first time in my life in a virgin forest, where the sound of the axe had never been heard.

I wandered along in delight, observing the blessings and ravages of time, which creates and destroys; I amused myself in tracing allthe periods of the life of an oak, from the moment it emerges from the earth with two small leaves, until nothing remains of it except a dark line, the dust of its heart.

Mr. King reproached me for my distraction, and we commenced our sport. We shot two or three of those small, delicate, fat, little grey partridges which are such tender eating. We then knocked down six or seven grey squirrels, which are much esteemed in the neighbourhood; ultimately our lucky star led us into a flock of wild turkeys.

They rose at a short interval, one after the other, making a great noise, flying fast and screaming. Mr. King fired at the first bird that rose, and followed it; the others were already out of shot, when a straggler rose; I took steady aim, and the bird fell dead.

It is only a sportsman who can feel the internal satisfaction I experienced at this shot. I grasped the noble bird, I turned it over and over on the ground, when I heard Mr. King hallooing to me to come and help him. I ran up, and found that all he wanted was to find his turkey, which he swore he had shot, but which had nevertheless disappeared.

I put my dog in, but he led us into such a thicket that a snake could scarcely have slided through; so we gave it up as a bad job, which put my comrade into a bad temper until he got home.

The rest of the days sport is not worth mentioning. We lost our way going back, and began to fancy we should have to sleep in the forest, when we heard the silver voices of the Misses Bulow, and the deep base of the father, who had been kind enough to issue forth to meet us.

The four sisters had got themselves up; fresh dresses, new sashes, pretty little bonnets, and such dandy shoes, showed they had taken some pains on our account; for my part, I determined to be as amiable as I could to the one who came and put her arm through mine with as much seeming right as if she had been my wife.

On reaching the farm we found supper ready; but before partaking of it we warmed ourselves for a few minutes before a blazing fire, lit on our account, although the weather did not require it. It did us much good, and roused us completely.

We ate like famished men; an ample bowl of punch crowned the entertainment, and the conversation of our host, who opened his heart more freely than on the previous evening, led us far into the night.

We spoke of the war of independence, where Mr. Bulow served as a superior officer; of M. de la Fayette, who holds a high footing in the hearts of the Americans, who always speak of him as the Marquis; of agriculture, which made profitable returns to America; and finally, of France, which I loved all the more from being compelled to leave it.

As interludes to the conversation, Mr. Bulow from time to time asked his eldest daughter Maria to sing. With a charming blush, she sang Yankee-doodle, the plaintive song of Mary Stuart, Major Andres lament, all popular in this part of the country. Maria had taken a few lessons, and was looked upon as a virtuosa, but what charmed me most was her simple, unaffected manner and rich voice.

We left on the morrow, despite the earnest entreaties to remain, for I had business to attend to. Whilst the horses were getting ready, Mr. Bulow took me aside, and made the following remarkable observations to me:–

"You behold in me, my dear sir, a happy man, if there is one under the canopy of heaven. All that you have seen is my own property. These stockings were knitted by my daughters; my shoes and clothes are made from my flocks; the latter provide me with ample food, and, to the praise of our government be it said, there are thousands of farmers as happy as I am, and whose doors, like mine, have no locks to them. Taxes here are nominal. As long as they are regularly paid, we may sleep in peace. Congress favours as much as possible our rising industry; agents continually visit us to purchase what we have to sell, and I have ready money in hand for a long time to come, as I have just sold my flour at twenty-four dollars per ton, the usual price having been eight. This is the result of the liberty which we have achieved and founded on sound laws. I am master here, and you will not be astonished when I tell you that the sound of the drum is never heard, and that, with the exception of the 4th of July, the glorious anniversary of our independence, neither soldiers, uniforms, nor bayonets are to be seen."

During the whole of the ride home I was lost in deep thought: the reader may perhaps fancy I was pondering on the allocution of Mr. Bulow, but I had far other thoughts to meditate upon. I was thinking how I should cook my turkey; and I was somewhat puzzled, for I feared I should not find at Hartford everything I required, for I wished to elevate a trophy by displaying my prey to advantage.

I make a painful sacrifice by suppressing the details of my intense labour, the object of which was to give a distinguand dinner to the Americans I invited. Let it suffice to say that I had the

H 2 wings of the partridges served up en papillate, and the grey squirrels stewed in Madeira,

As regards the turkey, the only roast we had, it was pleasing to the eye, nattering to the smell, and delicious to the taste. Thus, when the last particle had vanished, there was a universal murmur of applause, "Very good! exceedingly good! Oh! dear Sir! what a glorious bit!"

GAME.

Under the denomination " Game" we understand all animals fit to be eaten, which live in the woods and fields in a natural state of liberty.

We say "fit to be eaten," because some such animals do not come under the head of game: as foxes, badgers, crows, magpies, owls, andc.

Game may be divided into three classes:

The flesh of the wild turkey is darker and more perfumed than that of the domestic turkey.

I find that my esteemed friend M. Bosc shot some wild turkeys in Carolina, which he found excellent, and of a much better flavour than those we rear in Europe. He advises all rearers of turkeys to allow them as much liberty as possible, to take them out into the fields, and even into the woods; it will heighten their flavour, and bring them nearer the primitive species.

The first commences with the thrush, and comprises all lesser birds.

The second ranges higher, commencing with the corn-crake, then snipe, woodcock, partridge, pheasant, rabbit and hare. This is real game.

The third is better known as venison; it comprises the wild-boar, roe, deer, and all others of the hoof-footed species.

Game forms the charm of our dinners; it is wholesome, warm, savoury, of fine flavour, and easy of digestion to all young persons.

But these qualities are not so inherent as not to require some skill in their preparation. Throw into a pot a handful of salt, some water, and a piece of beef; you will have boiled beef and broth. If, instead of beef, you throw in wild-boar or venison, the beef will be far the best of the three.

But, in the hands of a clever cook, game undergoes a great many learned modifications and transformations, and provides the majority of the high savoury dishes which constitute " transcendent cookery."

The value of game also depends upon where it is killed. A red-partridge from Perigord has not the same flavour as a red-partridge from Sologne; and, whilst a hare shot in a field near Paris is but a poor dish, a leveret killed in the hills of Val-romey or of the Upper Dauphine is perhaps the most delicate of quadrupeds.

Amongst the little birds, the first in order of excellence is incontestably the becca-fica. It fattens as much as the ortolan, and nature has moreover endowed it with a slight bitterness, and so exquisite a flavour, that all the powers of taste are brought into play. If the becca-fica was as big as a pheasant, it would be cheap at an acre of land.

It is sad that this privileged little bird is so rarely seen at Paris; a few may be had there, but they are poor samples, not fat enough, in which their merit consists, and they will not bear comparison with those found in the South of France.

When I was a boy, I remember a story of one Father Fabi, a Jesuit, born in the diocese of Belley, who had a particular fancy for becca-ficas. As soon as they were cried, people exclaimed, "Behold the becca-ficas! Father Fabi is coming." And sure enough he never failed to arrive with a friend on the 1st of September; they regaled themselves upon them on the journey. Every one asked them to dinner, and they left on the 25th. As long as he was in France he never omitted this ornithophilite excursion, which was only interrupted when he was sent on a mission to Rome, where he died as penitentiary in 1688. Father Fabi was a man of deep learning; he wrote various works on theology and physics, in one of which he endeavours to prove that he discovered the circulation of the blood before, or at least as soon as, Harvey.

Few men know how to eat a little bird; I had the secret entrusted to me by Canon Charcot, a born gourmand and perfect gastronome, long before the latter word was adopted.

Take a fat little bird by the beak, sprinkle a little salt over it, take out the gullet, put the bird cleverly into your mouth, bite him off close to your fingers, and chew him manfully; the result will be an abundance of juice to envelope the whole organ, and you will enjoy a pleasure unknown to the vulgar.

"Odi profauum vulgus, et arceo."– Hot.

Amongst game proper, the quail is the most mignon and pleasant. A fat quail is pleasing by its taste, form, and colour. It is a mistake to serve up a quail otherwise than roasted, or en papillate, because its flavour evaporates quickly, and, if brought in contact with a fluid, is gone in a moment.

The snipe (or woodcock) is also a good bird, but few men know how fully to appreciate its value. A snipe is never in its full glory except when roasted before the eyes of the sportsman, and especially of the sportsman who has killed it; then it is perfect, and the mouth waters with delight.

Above these, and indeed above them all, the pheasant takes highest rank; but few mortals know how to serve it up.

A pheasant eaten within the first eight days after it has been shot, is not worth a partridge or a chicken, because its merit consists in its aroma.

Science has investigated the expansion of this aroma, and experience has proved it; and a pheasant kept till it is on the point of decomposition is a morsel worthy of the most exalted gourmands.

HOW TO COOK A PHEASANT.

The pheasant is an enigma, the key of which is only known to the adepts; they alone know how fully to enjoy it.

Every substance has its apogee of esculence; some attain it before their full development, as capers, asparagus, grey partridges, pigeons, andc.; others arrive at it when in the full bloom of the existence allotted to them, as melons, most fruits, mutton, beef, venison, and red partridges; finally, others when decomposition commences, and of these especially the pheasant.

This latter bird, if eaten within three days after it has been shot, has no peculiar flavour. It has not the delicacy of a fowl, nor the flavour of a quail.

Taken at the proper point, the flesh is tender, sublime, and of high flavour, partaking at once of poultry and venison.

This desirable point is when decomposition commences: then its aroma is developed. This moment manifests itself to the profane by a slight smell, and by a slight change of colour under the feathers in front; but the inspired guess it by a sort of instinct which acts on various occasions; for instance, a good cook knows at a glance when he ought to take his fowl off the spit.

When the pheasant has arrived at this state, it must be plucked, but not before. Small slices of firm and sound lard must then be stuck on to it (jpiqug).

It is by no means an indifferent matter as regards plucking a pheasant too soon. Founded experience has shown that those which have been left in their feathers had a finer flavour than) those plucked, either because the contact of the: air neutralises some portion of the aroma, or be-j cause a portion of the juices destined to nourish the feathers is absorbed.

Thus prepared, it has to be stuffed. This is done as follows:

Take two snipes; bone them, and clear them so as to make two lots; the first of the meat, the second of the liver and entrails.

Make a stuffing of the meat, cutting it up small with beef-marrow, cooked by steam, a little lard (rape), pepper, salt, fine herbs, and a sufficient quantity of good truffles to fill the inside of the pheasant.

You must be careful that the stuffing does not protrude, which is sometimes a difficulty, when the bird is rather far gone. But it can be done with a little skill, by attaching a crust of bread.

Then take a piece of toast, which must exceed the size of the pheasant two inches each way, and lay the pheasant upon it longways; then take the livers and entrails of the snipes, and pound them with two large truffles, an anchovy, a little lard, and a suitable piece of fresh butter.

Spread this paste equally over your toast, and then place the pheasant, prepared as above, over it, so that all the juice which issues from it whilst roasting may be soaked in.

When the pheasant is done, serve it up reclining gracefully on the toast, place slices of lemon round, and you need not be anxious for the result.

This high-flavoured dish ought to be washed down with Burgundy (vin du cru de la Haute-Bourgogne). I arrived at this truth after a long series of observations, which gave me as much labour as going through Euclid.

A pheasant thus cooked is worthy of the table of the noblest in the land.

I saw one cooked by that worthy chef Picard, at the Chateau-de-la-Grange, at my charming friends Madame de Ville-Plaine. It was brought up in solemn procession by Louis, the major-domo. It was examined as minutely as a new bonnet from Madame Herbaults; it was smelt with anticipations of delight; and during this learned investigation the eyes of the ladies twinkled like stars, their lips became the colour of coral, and their features beamed with delight.

A pheasant thus dressed is called faisan a la Sainte-Alliance.

On another occasion, I had one served up to a board of magistrates of the Supreme Court, who know that it is necessary at times to put off senatorial dignity, and to whom I proved, without much difficulty, that good cheer is the natural compensation for the ennuis of the cabinet. After a suitable examination, the senior judge, in a serious voice pronounced the word "excellent!" All the others bowed consent, and the judgment passed unanimously.

During the deliberation, I had observed that the noses of these venerable senators gave very evident twitches of satisfaction, their brow was calm and serene, and a semi-smile hovered on their lips.

However, these marvellous effects are in the nature of things. A pheasant, cooked according to the above receipt, already a noble bird itself, becomes impregnated externally with the savoury fat of the lard, which carbonises; inside, it becomes impregnated with the odorous gases which escape from the snipe and truffle. The toast, already so well provided, receives a triple supply of juices from the bird whilst roasting.

Thus, of all these assembled good things, not an atom escapes appreciation, and considering the excellence of this dish, I deem it worthy of the table of the most august.

"Parve, nee invideo, sine me, liber, ibis in aulara."

FISH.

Some wiseacres have maintained that the Ocean was the common cradle of every living thing; that even man was born in the sea, and that his actual state is only due to the action of air and to the habits he was obliged to assume in this new element.

However this may be, it is at least certain that the empire of water contains an immense quantity of living things of every form and shape, which enjoy vital functions in various degrees, and on a system which is not the same as that of warm-blooded animals.

It is no less true that it offers an enormous mass of food, and that, in the present state of science, it provides our table with most agreeable variety.

Fish, less nourishing than meat, more succulent than vegetables, is a mezzo-termine which suits nearly every temperament, and may be even allowed to convalescents.

The Greeks and Eomans, though less advanced than us in the art of preparing fish, nevertheless held it in high esteem, pushing their refinement so far as to discover by the taste in what waters it had been caught. They kept them in tanks or in fish-ponds; and history records the cruelty of Vadius Pollion, who fed his eels with the bodies of slaves he had slain for the purpose—an act of cruelty which the Emperor Domitian highly disapproved, but which he ought to have punished-

A great discussion has arisen as to whether sea-fish or fresh-water fish ought to bear the palm of superiority. The question, doubtless, will never be decided, as the Spanish proverb has it, "Sobre los gustos no hai disputa" (Every man his own taste). No defined character can be given to these fugitive sensations, and there is no scale to judge whether a cod-fish, a sole, or turbot, is better than a salmon-trout or a tench of six or seven pounds.

It has been generally agreed that fish contains less nourishment than meat, either because it does not contain any osmazome, or beoause, being lighter in weight, it contains less volume in the same space. Shell-fish, especially oysters, contain very little nutritious matter; this is why a large quantity may be eaten before dinner without interfering with the repast which follows immediately.

It may be remembered that not very long since every dinner commenced with oysters, and that many of the guests swallowed some few dozen, even as many as twelve dozen. I wished to ascertain the weight of this avant-garde, and I found that a dozen oysters (water included) weigh four ounces, or twelve dozen three pounds. This satisfied me that the same men who eat a hearty dinner afterwards, would have been completely appeased, had they eaten the same quantity of meat, even of chicken. Whilst at Versailles, in 1798, as commissary for the Directory, I was brought continually in contact with Sieur Laperte, greffier of the tribunal, a great amateur of oysters. He said he never yet had been able to eat enough at one sitting, or, as he expressed it, " tout son soul."

I resolved to procure him that satisfaction, and I invited him to dinner.

He came. I kept time with him up to the third dozen, when I let him go on alone. He had eaten thirty-two dozen; the operation taking an hour, the person who opened them being rather slow; and as I had not dined, I stopped him when he appeared only in full swing: " Mon cher," I said, " it is not your fate to eat your soul of oysters today. Let us dine!" We did so, and he made as hearty a dinner as if he had been fasting.

The ancients extracted two sorts of seasoning from fishes, muria and garum.

The first was simply brine of the tunny, or, to define it closer, the liquid substance which the mixture of salt caused to run from off the fish.

Garum, which brought a much higher price, is not so well known to us. It is supposed to have been taken by pressure from the entrails of the scomber, or mackerel; but, then, why its high price? There is reason to believe it was some foreign sauce; perhaps nothing else than soy, which we import from India, and which consists of the result of fish fermented with mushrooms.

Some races, from their peculiar position, are doomed to live almost entirely upon fish; they also feed their cattle with them, which become accustomed to this unusual food; they manure their land with fish, and yet the sea which surrounds them never ceases to provide them always with the same quantity.

It has been observed that such races do not possess so much courage as beef-eating nations; they are pale, which is not surprising, because, according to the elements of which fish consists, it is more calculated to increase the lymph than repair the blood.

Numerous examples of longevity have been observed among ichthyophagi. This may be attri buted either to the fact of light and unsubstantial food obviating apoplexy, or that the juices it contains, being only destined by nature to form bones and gristle, the growth is retarded, and takes a longer time in the development of all those parts of the body, the solidification of which becomes finally the cause of death.

However this may be, fish, in the hands of a good cook, may become an inexhaustible source of enjoyment; it is served up whole, in pieces, boiled, fried, a fhuile, in wine, hot, or cold; and it is always well received; but it never deserves so warm a reception as when served up as a matelote.

Analytic gastronomy has endeavoured to examine the effects of a fish regimen on the animal economy. The results obtained are concordant, and must have doubtless been ignored by those ecclesiastical legislators, who ordered that fish should be eaten as a fast at least four days in the week.

Eegarded as a species, fish offers to the philosopher an inexhaustible source of meditation and wonder. The varied forms of these strange creatures, the senses they are wanting in, the limited ones they possess, the influence which the dif ference of the centre in which they are doomed to live, to breathe and move, must have exercised upon all this, extend the sphere of our ideas, and of the indefinite modifications which may result from the matter and movement of life. As for myself, I entertain for fishes a sentiment which borders upon respect, and which arises from the intimate conviction that they are evidently antediluvian creatures; the great cataclysm, which drowned our grand-uncles about the eighteenth century of the creation of the world, must have been for fishes a time of rejoicing, of conquest, and festivity.

TRUFFLES.

Whoever says " Truffle," pronounces a grand word which arouses at once the feelings of both sexes.

The origin of the truffle is unknown. It is found, but whence it is derived is still a secret. The most skilful men of science have endeavoured to analyse it, hoping to get the seed, so as to sow and reap. Vain efforts! deluded hopes! No crop rewarded their labour; and this is perhaps no great evil; for as the price of truffles is somewhat a fancy one, they would perhaps be esteemed less if plentiful and cheap.

"Eejoice, my dear Madam," I once said to Madame de V–, "an invention has just been presented to the Society of Encouragement, by means of which the finest lace can be made almost for nothing." "What!" replied the fair lady, with a look of sovereign indifference, " if lace was cheap, do you suppose we should wear such rubbish?"

The truffle was known to the Eomans; but the French sort does not seem to have reached them. They imported truffles from Greece, Africa, and chiefly from Libya; they had a white and pink appearance; those from Libya were most sought after, and had the finest flavour.

Gustus elementa per omnia quaerunt. (Juvenal.)

From the Eomans down to our own days there was a long interregnum, and the resurrection of truffles is of a recent date; I have waded through many receipt books, where no mention is made of them; it may even be asserted that the generation, which is about to pass away, witnessed it.

About 1780, truffles were rare at Paris; they were to be had only, and in small quantity, at the Hotel des Americains" and " Hotel de Provence;" a truffled turkey was a piece of luxury, only to be found on the table of noble lords or of kept women.

We are indebted to the green-grocers for the increased supply of truffles. Perceiving that they were1 sought after, and were well paid, they had them brought by the mail, and paid agents to procure them.

In 1825 the glory of the truffle may be said to have reached its culminating point; no good dinner was without its piece truffee, no entree, however good, is perfect without truffles. Whose mouth does not water at the announcement of " truffes a laprovenyale?"

A saute de truffes is always placed before the lady of the house, who does the honours: in short the truffle is the " diamond" of the cuisine.

Peculiar qualities have been attributed to truffles. I will only give one anecdote which, gentle reader, you had better not read.

I questioned an old lady friend of mine, whether there was any truth in the common opinion that truffles had an influence upon the heart. She gave me as a reply the following anecdote:– ." Sir," she said, " in the days when suppers were still the fashion, I was supping one day en trio with my husband and one of his friends. Verseuil (that was his name) was a handsome young man, not devoid of wit, and a constant visitor at our house; but he had never said anything to me to make me fancy he wanted to make love; and when he did pay me little attentions they were paid with so much good nature that a woman must have been a fool to have heeded them. It seems that this evening we were destined to be alone, as my husband had an appointment on business. Our supper was light, but we had a superb vo-laille truffee, sent to me as a present by the sub-delegate of Perigueux. At that day it was a rare present. The truffles were delicious, and, as you know, I love them; but I was moderate, and drank only one glass of champagne; I had that presentiment that something unusual was going to happen which is a peculiar instinct in women. My husband left us very early, leaving me alone with Verseuil. Conversation went on on everyday subjects, but it soon partook of a more familiar turn. Verseuil made himself most agreeable, and perceiving that I only laughed at his pretty sayings he became animated. I woke as from a dream. I was obliged to be severe to stop him. He left, and I went to bed, when I fell at once into a deep sleep. When I awoke in the morning I meditated upon what had passed, and reproached myself with want of energy. I ought to have stopped him at once, pulled the bell, and done everything which I did not do. Well, Sir, I attribute it all to the truffles–and I never eat them afterwards without being on my guard."

This frank avowal by no means lays down. a law. I made deep investigations, and the result is that I believe truffles have a peculiar influence upon the more tender feelings of the human species.

White truffles are found in Piedmont, and they are much esteemed; they have a slight smack of garlic, which is, however, not disagreeable, as it does not remain. The best French truffles come from Perigord and Upper Provence; they are in full flavour in January. They are also found at Bugey, but they do not keep. I tried at four different times to have them at Paris, but the attempt only succeeded once. Truffles from Bour-gogne and the Dauphine are of inferior quality; they are tough and tasteless.

There are " truffles " and " truffles."

Dogs and pigs are trained especially to discover, truffles; but there are men whose eye is so correct they can tell at a glance where truffles are to be found, and they can even predict their size and quality.

Is the truffle indigestible?

We say, no. And we come to this decision on the following grounds:– 1. It is easily chewed: is light of weight 2. During an observation of fifty years we have never known a regular truffle-eater suffer from indigestion.

3. We have the same judgment from the most celebrated practitioners in Paris, a city devoted to truffles par excellence.

4. Finally, those learned doctors eat more truffles themselves than any one else. I need only mention Dr. Malouet who absorbed a sufficient quantity to give an elephant an indigestion.

I, therefore, maintain that the truffle is nutritious as well as agreeable, and taken with moderation is like a letter slipped in at the post-office.

It is true that a man may feel unwell after a great dinner at which truffles were served up. But this only happens to men who cram themselves with a host of other good things. Had they afterwards eaten as many potatoes as truffles the result would have been the same.

It is so very easy to be mistaken as to the cause of indigestion. One day I asked to dinner an old gentleman, Mr. S, a noted bon-vivant.

Whether it was that I knew his tastes, or that I wished to prove to my guests that I had their happiness at heart, I was lavish in truffles. I had a magnificent turkey admirably stuffed.

M. S did full justice to it. On reaching home he was taken with violent spasms. A doctor was sent for, and the symptoms became. so serious that some alarm was felt. Suddenly nature came to the rescue. He opened his mouth and shot out a fragment of truffle intact, which bounded back from the wall. The bad symptoms ceased immediately. Poor S -a teeth, which had been doing service for many years, were not quite up to their work; some had emigrated and others were not so firm as they should have been. The fragment had stuck in the pylorus. There was no indigestion. He fell into a comfortable sleep, was perfectly well next day, and attacked truffles with as much energy afterwards as ever, taking care, however, to masticate them more carefully.

Poets have not been wanting to sing the glories of the truffle: the following " impromptu" was written by M. B. de V, a distinguished amateur:–

Buvons a la truffe noire,
Et ne soyons point ingrats;
Elle assure la Yictoire
Dans les plus charmans combats.
Au seeours
Des amours,
Du plaisir la Providence
Envoya cette substance;
Quon en serve tous les jours.

8UGAH.

In the advanced state of science of the present day, we understand by Sugar a substance, sweet to the taste, susceptible of crystallisation, and which by fermentation is dissoluble into carbonic acid and alcohol.

Sugar, as formerly understood, was the arundo saccharifera, the thick crystallised sugar of the cane.

The sugar-cane is a native plant of India; nevertheless it is true that the Eomans did not use sugar habitually. There are a few passages in ancient authors which may lead to the supposi- tion that a sweet juice had been discovered in certain reeds. Lucan says:–

"Quique bibunt tenera dulces ab arundine succos," but as regards sugar as we now have it, the Eomans were totally ignorant.

It has been brought to perfection step by step, and has become a most important article of commerce; it is a source of fortune to the cultivator and the trader, and for the governments that levy a tax upon it.

For some time it was supposed that the heat of the tropics was requisite for the production of sugar; but about the year 1740, Margraff discovered it in various plants of the temperate zone, more especially in beet-root. The investigations of Professor Achard of Berlin confirmed the fact.

The events at the commencement of the nineteenth century having rendered sugar scarce and dear in France, investigations were set on foot by the government. The result was that sugar was discovered to exist in the grape, chestnut, and potato, but more especially in the beet-root.

The cultivation of the beet-root became quite a separate branch, and manufactories of beet-root sugar sprang up in various parts of France. On the restoration of peace, when the price of colonial sugar fell, the beet-root manufactories declined. A vulgar idea-perfectly erroneous–got abroad, that beet-root sugar was not so good as colonial sugar. Science has proved its fallacy.

Eau sucree is a refreshing beverage, wholesome, agreeable, and sometimes salutary as a remedy.

It is made use of for syrups, ices, (which were introduced by Catherine de Medici) liqueurs, biscuits, creams, blanc-manger, according to the liquids with which it is mixed. Mixed with coffee it brings out the aroma. Preserves, marmalades, candies, all depend upon it. In fact its use is general.

COFFEE.

Coffee pounded in a mortar is much more aromatic Than ground as is usual. The Turks make the best coffee.

That coffee has an effect upon the brain there can be no doubt. A man who takes coffee for the first time is sure to be deprived of a portion of his sleep.

Voltaire and Buffon took a great deal of coffee; it is not improbable that they are ndebted thereto, the first for the admirable lucidity observable in his writings, the latter for the enthusiastic harmony of his style. It is evident ttat his treatises on "Man" "the Dog"–" the Tiger "–" the Lion " and the Horse" were written in a state of extraordinary cerebral exaltation.

The wakefulness caused by coffee is not painful; the intellect is clear, but there is no desire to sleep. That is all. Yet, in the long-run it may prove noxious.

I recommend all mothers not to allow their growing children to drink coffee. It curtails their growth and makes mummies of them.

The Duke of Massa, when Minister of Justice, asked me to do some work for him which I knew would occupy the whole night, and it was to be done at once. I took two strong cups of coffee after dinner. I returned home at seven oclock, but instead of the papers I found a letter to say that owing to unforeseen circumstances I should not receive them till the next day.

I returned to the house where I had dined, and played two or three rubbers. I returned home and went to bed, hoping that I should have a few hours sleep at least.

In vain. My head became clearer; I was in a violent state of mental agitation. I got up, and put a little story, which I had read the previous day, into verse. But sleep would not come. I never shut an eye all night nor next day. I remained forty hours without sleep.

CHOCOLATE.

The first men who landed in America were urged by the thirst for gold. At that period almost the only value recognised was that extracted from mines; agriculture and commerce were in their infancy, and political economy still unborn. The Spaniards discovered precious metals,–a sterile discovery, as it depreciates in proportion as it multiplies when compared to the other active means to add to riches.

But those lands where a sun of every degree of heat gives extreme fecundity to the earth, were proper for the cultivation of coffee; moreover the potato, indigo, vanille, cocoa, andc., were discovered there. Those are the real riches of the country.

If these discoveries took place despite the barriers opposed to curiosity by a jealous nation, it may reasonably be hoped that in succeeding years they will be tenfold and that the investigations of scientific men of Europe in unexplored lands will enrich the three kingdoms with a multitude of new substances, which will give us new sensations, as did vanille, and will increase our alimentary resources like the cocoa.

It has been agreed to call chocolate the mixture which results from the bean of the cocoa roasted with sugar and cinnamon. Sugar is an integral part, for with cocoa alone you can only make cocoa paste and not chocolate. When vanille is added to the sugar, cocoa, and cinnamon, we have the ne plus ultra of the composition.

The cocoa-tree is a product of South America; it is found on the islands and on the main land; the trees which grow on the banks of the Maracaibo, in the valleys of Caracas, and in the rich province of Sokonusco are esteemed the best, the berry is larger, the juice less acid, and the aroma finer. Since those countries have become more accessible it has been able to form a comparison; and an exercised palate is never deceived.

The Spanish ladies of the New World are fond of chocolate to excess. Not satisfied with taking it two or three times a day they even have it sometimes brought to them in church. For this they have often been reproved by the bishops. But they finally winked at it, and the venerable father, Escobar, whose metaphysics were as subtile as his morals were accommodating, formally declared that chocolate a, Ieau did not interfere with fasting, quoting the old adage, "Liqui-dum non frangit jejunium."

Chocolate was introduced into Spain about the seventeenth century; it became soon popular by the decided predilection shown for it by the priesthood and the women. The taste still prevails, and throughout the whole of the Peninsula at the present day it is customary to offer chocolate as refreshment to a visitor.

Chocolate crossed the mountains with Anne of Austria, daughter of Philip II., and wife of Louis XIII. The Spanish monks also introduced it by the presents they sent to their brethren in France. The different Spanish ambassadors also brought it into use: and at the commencement of the Eegency it was in more general use than coffee, because then it was taken as agreeable food, whilst coffee was only sipped as a luxury and a curiosity.

Linnaeus styles cocoa, cacao theobroma, or "drink of the gods." Attempts have been made to discover the reason for so strong a denomination; some attribute it to the fact that he was passionately fond of chocolate; others that he wished to please his confessor; others out of gallantry to please a Queen who had introduced it.

Chocolate has been the subject of deep dissertations, with a view to determine its nature and properties, and to place it in the category of hot, cold, or temperate food; it must be owned that these learned documents have served but little to the establishment of the truth.

But time and experience, those two great masters, have established that chocolate, carefully prepared, is as wholesome as it is agreeable; that it is nutritious and easy of digestion; that it does not hurt the complexion as coffee is supposed to do, on the contrary, it clears it; that it is well suited to men of all sedentary or mental occupations, to literary men, barristers, and travellers; finally, that it will not hurt the weakest stomachs; that it has proved beneficial in chronic diseases, and becomes the last resource in affections of the pylorus.

Chocolate is indebted for these various properties to the fact of being an eleosac-charum; there are few substances which contain in equal volume so many nutritious particles.

During the war, cocoa was scarce, and very dear; attempts were made to replace it, but all in vain; one of the benefits of peace was, to deliver us from the many concoctions, which were as much chocolate as chicory is coffee.

Some people complain they cannot digest chocolate; others, on the contrary, pretend that it does not contain sufficient nourishment, and digests too soon.

It is very probable that the first have only themselves to blame, and that they purchase bad chocolate; good chocolate will not offend the most delicate stomach. As regards the others, the remedy is easy; let them have a chop or a kidney with it, and let them thank Heaven for giving them a strong digestion.

I will now mention a fact which is the result of observation.

After having made a hearty and excellent breakfast, swallow a cup of good choco-late, and within three hours the digestive organs will have performed their functions. From zeal for the science, I requested various ladies to try it; they first said they should die, but found it answer so well that they glorified the professor.

Persons who take chocolate, generally speaking, enjoy constant good health; they are less subject to a host of little ills which jar upon the K happiness of life; their em-bonpoint remains the same; these two advantages may be verified in society amongst those whose regimen is known.

In Spain, they make very good chocolate; Italian chocolate is not so pleasant to the taste, the berry being generally overroasted, which gives a bitter flavour.

To make good chocolate, dissolve about an ounce and a half, for one cup, in water heated gradually, stirring it with a wooden spoon. Let it boil for a quarter of an hour, and serve up hot.

CHAP. VIII.

HOW TO FRY.

It was a fine May day; the sun shed its warm rays on the roofs of the houses of the great city of delights, and the streets (a rare occurrence) were free from mud and dust.

The heavy diligences had, for some time, ceased to shake the pavement; luggage vans were silent, and only a few open carriages, full of fair ladies with elegant bonnets, passed at intervals.

It was three oclock in the afternoon, when the professor sat down in his arm chair to meditate. His right leg rested vertically on the carpet; his extended left leg formed a diagonal; his back reposed comfortably on the cushions, and his hands rested on the lion heads that adorn the arms of that venerable household relic. His elevated brow indicated deep thought, and his mouth betrayed amiable distractions. His whole attitude was one of meditation; and any one beholding him would have mentally observed: That is a sage!

Thus established, the professor sent for his head cook; and shortly he entered, ready to receive advice, lessons, or orders.

"Maitre la Planche," said the professor, with that grave accent which penetrates every heart, " every man who dines at my table proclaims you a potagiste de premiere classe: that is well, for the potage is the first consolation of a hungry stomach; but I am sorry to find that you have much to learn in the art of frying.

"I heard you sigh yesterday, when that magnificent sole was served up pale, soft, and discoloured. My friend B shot a glance of disapprobation towards you; M. H. E. turned his gnomonic nose to the west, and President S. deplored the failure as a public calamity.

"This misfortune has befallen you for having neglected theory, the full importance of which you do not appreciate. You are a little obstinate, and I have some difficulty in making you understand that the phenomena which take place in your laboratory are nothing else than the execution of the eternal laws of nature; and that certain things which you do carelessly, simply because you have seen others do so, emanate, nevertheless, from the highest abstractions of science.

"Listen to me, then, with attention, and learn, that you may not again have to blush at your performance.

"Liquids exposed to the action of fire do not all attain the same degree of heat; nature has made them unequal in this respect; it is an order of things, the secret of which she reserves, and which we call calorific capacity.

"Thus, you may with impunity dip your finger in boiling spirits of wine;. you would draw it out very quickly from brandy; still quicker from water, and a rapid immersion in boiling oil would make a cruel wound, for oil is capable of three times the heat of water.

"It is consequent upon this disposition that boiling liquids act differently upon sapid bodies thrown into them. Those put into water become soft, dissolve, and form a soup; those, on the contrary, put into oil, condense, acquire a hue more or less brown, and end by carbonising.

"In the former case, the water dissolves, and extracts the internal juices of the substances thrown in; in the latter, those juices are preserved, because oil cannot dissolve them; if those substances dry up, it is because a continuation of the heat finally makes them evaporate in humidity.

"The two methods have also different names; the process of boiling substances intended for the table in oil or grease is called frying. I think I have already explained to you that oil and grease are almost synonymous, grease being simply condensed oil, and oil liquid grease.

"Fried things are pleasant dishes; they make a tasty variation. The whole merit consists in the formation of the crust, or, to use the proper word, la surprise. To do this well, the boiling liquid must be sufficiently hot for its action to be sudden and instantaneous; it requires a good well-kept-up fire to procure this result. To ascertain whether the liquid is hot enough, dip a piece of bread into the frying-pan and keep it there for five or six seconds; if you withdraw it firm and coloured, make your fry at once; if not, stir your fire and try it again. The surprise or immersion once done, moderate your fire that the juices thus imprisoned may undergo, under a prolonged heat, the change which unites them and enhances their flavour.

"You will, doubtless, have observed that the surface of well-fried objects will not dissolve either salt or sugar, which, nevertheless, they need according to their peculiar nature. Therefore you must reduce both those aggrediants to the finest powder, and use a sprinkling box.

"I will not tell you what oil or grease to use; your library contains sufficient books on that subject.

"However, you must not forget that when you have to fry trout, which scarcely exceed a quarter of a pound, which have been caught in some running stream, you must take the very best olive oil; this simple dish, well fried and adorned with slices of lemon, is worthy to be offered to a Cardinal.

"A Neapolitan, dining with me one day when I had this dish, exclaimed, Questo and un vero boccone di Cardmale. Why, I retorted, dont you say a dish for a King? My dear Sir, he replied, we Italians do not believe that kings are gourmets; their repasts are too short and too solemn; but Cardinals! eh!!! and he chuckled with delight, Hou hou, hou hou, hou hou!

"Cook smelts in the same way. They are the beccafica of the water; same smallness, same perfume, same superiority.

These two prescriptions are also founded on the nature of things, and experience has taught that olive oil should only be used for operations which can be quickly done, or that do not require great heat.

"You took charge of my lower regions, and you were the first man to serve up an immense turbot, fried. Great was the joy that day amongst the elect!

"Go, continue to give your usual attention to everything; but do not forget that as soon as the guests arrive in my salon, their whole happiness is in our hands."

CHAP. IX.

THIBST.

A Man dies much sooner of thirst than he does of hunger. Men who have been provided with water have been known to live for eight days without eating, whilst a man without beverage cannot live beyond five.

The reason of this difference is, that the latter dies of exhaustion and weakness, whilst the former suffers from a burning fever, which increases till he dies.

Water is the only beverage which really appeases thirst. This is why we drink very little of it. All other drinks are simply palliatives. If a man drank nothing but water, he could never "Kave been accused of drinking without being thirsty.

Beverages have one peculiar quality; they have immediate effect, and give immediate relief. Give a worn-out man the most substantial food; he will turn from it with disgust: pour a glass of wine or brandy down his throat; he will revive.

There is a curious fact well worthy of remark, namely, that sort of instinct, as general as it is imperious, which makes us desire strong drink.

Wine, the most pleasant of beverages, whether we are indebted for it to Noah who planted the vine, or to Bacchus who squeezed out the juice of the grape, dates from the childhood of the world; and beer, attributed to Osiris, goes back to times beyond certainty.

All men, even savages, have been so tormented by this thirst for strong drink, that they have procured it however limited their knowledge.

They have soured the milk of their domestic animals; they have extracted the juice of fruits and roots, and have stumbled upon the elements of fermentation. And wherever we go in society we find men provided with strong drink. They use it at their feasts, their sacrifices, their marriages, their burials, in fact at every solemnity.

For centuries wine was drunk and sung before it was supposed that spirit, which gave it its strength, could be extorted from it. But the Arabs having taught us the art of distillation which they had discovered to extract perfume from flowers, more especially from the rose, so celebrated in their writings, it occurred that the flavour of wine might be extracted, and, step by step alcohol, spirits of wine, brandy, were extracted.

Alcohol is the monarch of liquids. America was subjugated by alcohol as much as by gunpowder.

This thirst for a liquid which nature has wrapped in mystery, this extraordinary desire traceable in every race of man, in every clime, under every temperature, is well worthy the attention of the philosophic observer.

I have pondered over it as others have done, and I am inclined to place the desire for fermented liquors side by side with anxiety for the future, for both are unknown to the brute creation, and I regard them as distinctive features of the master-piece of the last sublunary revolution.

CHAP. X.

LA GOURMANDISE.

We have no equivalent in the English language for the word " gourmandise" or " gourmand." " Epicurism" and epicure are perhaps the nearest approach. It is curious that Savarin throughout his work makes use of the expression " gourmand" to denote a refined eater. The French language possesses another definition, which Eoget would do well to insert into the next edition of his " Thesaurus" viz. Gourmet.

Our English idea of a "gourmand" is a man. who has a voracious appetite, likes good things, and swallows them wholesale; in fact–a glutton. Savarins "gourmand" is the "man of taste" as defined in Aphorism II.:

"Animals feed; man eats; it is only the man of intellect who knows how to eat."

I allude to the sixth edition of this valuable work; perhaps it may be in a later one.

Henceforth, then, gentle reader, remember that in these pages " gourmand "and " gourmandise "imply the refinement of the " Art of Dining."

Social "gourmandise" combines the elegance of Athens with the luxury of Eome and the refinement of Paris. It implies intellect, taste, and judgment. It is a passionate preference which grows upon man for objects which flatter his taste.

Gourmandise is the very reverse of gluttony; it is the enemy of every excess. A man who eats till he gets an indigestion, or who gets drunk, is immediately struck off the list of " gourmands."

Gourmandise comprises refined taste for the most delicate dishes, even preserves and pastry. It admits women into its ranks. In whatever light you look upon it, it is deserving of praise and encouragement.

In a physical point of view it is the result and proof of a healthy and perfect state of the organs destined for nutrition. In a moral point of view it is an implicit resignation to the behests of the Creator, who having ordained that we should eat to live, invites us thereto by appetite, supports us by taste, and rewards us by pleasure.

In the point of view of political economy,"gourmandise" is the common link which unites nations by the reciprocal exchange of articles of daily use. It sends wines from pole to pole; brandy, sugar, groceries, and provisions of every description, even to eggs and melons, are all at its command. It regulates the price of good and bad articles of food according to their respective merits. It keeps up the emulation of sportsmen, fishermen, and gardeners, whose labours adorn the tables of the rich.

Finally, it gives employment to a host of cooks, pastry-cooks, confectioners, and others, beyond calculation.

In the present state of society, it would be difficult to imagine a people living exclusively on bread and vegetables. If such a nation existed, it would infallibly be subjugated by a carnivorous army, as the Hindoos have successively fallen a prey to all who attacked them, or else it would be converted by the cuisine of its neighbours in like manner as the Bosotians became gourmands after the battle of Leuctra.

There is not an equivalent for the word cuisine in the English language.

To the Exchequer " gourmandise" is a godsend. Everything good we eat is taxed, and " gourmands "are the main support of the Treasury.

What saved France from bankruptcy in 1815?–"La gourmandise"

When the Allies entered Paris, the sums they spent paid the indemnity. Very made his fortune; Achard commenced his; Beauvilliers made a third fortune; and Madame Sullot of the Palais Eoyal sold 12,000 petits pates daily.

When the army entered Champagne, it took 600,000 bottles of wine from the renowned cellars of M. Moet depernay. The owner consoled himself for the loss when he found the pillagers retained the taste of his wine, and the orders he afterwards received amply compensated him for the robbery.

Gourmandise is not confined to the male sex. There is nothing so agreeable to behold as a " pretty gourmande." Her napkin is well placed; one of her hands rests on the table; the other armed with a fork conveys delicate little morsels to. her mouth; her eyes sparkle; her lips are vermilion; her conversation is agreeable; every movement is graceful; she is not wanting in that clever coquet-terie which a clever woman knows so well how to turn to account. With such advantages, she is irresistible; and Cato the Censor himself would be moved.

The inclination of the fair sex for good-living is a natural instinct, because it is favourable to their good looks.

A series of observations has convinced me that ladies who live well remain younger much longer than others.

It gives more brilliancy to the eye, more freshness to the skin, more support to the muscles; and, as physiology has proved that the depression of the muscles causes wrinkles, those dreaded enemies of beauty; it is also true, taking all on an equal footing, that the ladies who know how to eat are, comparatively, ten years younger than those who are ignorant on the subject.

Painters and sculptors are well aware of this truth, for they never paint or chisel a miser or an anchorite without making them appear pale, wrinkled, and miserable.

Coquetry is a bad translation; we have no equivalent in the English language.

La gourmandise is one of the great links which keeps society together; it gradually ex-. tends that spirit of conviviality which daily unites various classes, amalgamates them, animates the conversation, and rounds off the sharp corners of conventional inequality.

It also makes it incumbent upon the man who asks his friends to dinner, to have a care to their comforts; and the latter feel grateful at finding they have been well taken care of.

Eternal shame to those stupid feeders who bolt down with indifference the most delicate morsels, and who gulp first-rate wines without tasting

Every well-bred man may pay a delicate compliment to the host who has done his best to please him.

It is not every man that is born a " gourmand."

There are individuals to whom nature has de nied that delicate formation of organs without which they are incapable of appreciating the most savoury morsels. There is another class of men who are bad eaters. Absent-minded, business men, ambitious men, who wish to do two things at once, and think whilst they eat, and who only eat to satisfy their cravings.

Napoleon I. was one of this class; he was irregular in his meals, and ate hastily and badly; but he displayed in this matter that same absolute will he exercised in everything else. As soon as he felt an appetite he must be satisfied; and his attendants had strict orders to be ready at any moment to give him chicken, cutlets, or coffee.

But there is a privileged class whom a material and organic predestination calls to the enjoyments of taste.

I was always a disciple of Lavater and Gall. I believe in innate dispositions.

As some individuals come into the world evidently with bad sight, a distorted walk, or bad ears, so are they blind, lame, and deaf. Why then should not certain individuals be predisposed to experience in a higher degree certain series of sensations. Moreover, with a little observation, you may, at every moment, discover men in society who bear upon their countenance the marked stamp of some ruling passion. When a face bears this mark it is rarely deceptive.

Passions act on the nervous system, and often though a man is silent you may read in his face what is passing in his mind. This tension of the muscles, if habitual, soon leaves sensible traces, and gives a permanent and recognisable character to the countenance.

Gourmands by predestination are generally of the middle height: they have round or square faces (carrand), sparkling eyes, small forehead, short nose, full lips, and round chins. The women are dimpled, pretty rather than handsome, with an inclination to embonpoint.

Those who are especially addicted to good eating, have finer features, a more refined appearance; they are more mignonnes, and are distinguished by a peculiar manner of their own in swallowing. Under this exterior the most amiable dinner-companions are to be found: they partake of every dish handed to them, eat slowly, and taste with reflection. They are in no hurry to leave the spot where they have been well enter-

Tasso well describes this voluptuous lip:–

"Quel labbro, che le rose ban colorito,
Molle si sporge e tumidetto in fuore,
Spinto per arte, mi cred io d amore,
A fare ai baci insidioso invito."

"That lip, which (like the rose that morn with dew
Has largely fed), so moist, so sweetly swells;
That lip approaches thus, by Cupids spells,
To tempt to kiss, and still that kiss renew."

L 2 tallied, and you have them for the rest of the evening, because they are aware what games and amusements are to follow the ordinary accessories of a gastronomic meeting.

Those, on the contrary, to whom nature has denied an aptitude for the enjoyments of taste, have long faces, long noses, and long eyes; no matter what their stature, there is something longitudinal about them. They have sleek black hair, and are thin and lanky: it is they who invented trowsers.

Women, whom nature has similarly afflicted, are angulous, yawn at dinner, and live upon whist and scandal.

I do not fear many contradictions to this physiological theory, because any man can verify its truth for himself; I shall, however, support it by two or three examples.

I was sitting one day at a large dinner, and had opposite to me a very pretty person, whose whole figure denoted sensuality. I whispered to my neighbour that with such features she must be a gourmande. "What nonsense!" he replied; " she is scarcely fifteen; that is not yet the age for gourmandise." However, let us watch her. The commencement was not at all favourable to me: I began to fear I had compromised myself: during the two first courses the young lady was abstemious to a degree. This discretion astonished me, and I feared I had stumbled upon an excep-. tional case, for " nulla regula sine exceptione. "But a magnificent dessert was served up, and this revived my hope. I was not deceived: not only did she eat of everything offered to her, but asked for dishes farthest off from her. She tasted everything; my neighbour was astonished where she could put so much. My diagnostic was verified, and once again science triumphed.

Two years afterwards, I met the same person; she had been recently married; she had grown up into a beautiful woman; slightly coquettish, she displayed all her charms to the best advantage. She was ravissante. Her husband was a picture. He looked like that celebrated ventriloquist, who could laugh on one side of his face, and cry on the other. He appeared much pleased that his wife was so much admired, but as soon as he thought an admirer was too warm in his attentions, a cold shiver of jealousy visibly pervaded his frame. The last sentiment prevailed. He hurried off his wife under his arm, and I never saw them again.

On another occasion, I made a similar observation on Duke Decres, for a long time minister of marine. He was short, stout, fair, broad shouldered; his face was nearly round, with rounded chin, full lips, and the mouth of a giant. I at once declared him a predestined amateur of good cheer.

I whispered my physiognomical observation into the ear of a pretty lady, who, I thought, was discreet. Alas! I was deceived. She was a daughter of Eve, and my secret would have choked her. That very evening his Excellency was informed of the scientific induction I had drawn from the ensemble of his features.

I learnt this on the following morning, in a very amiable letter from the duke, modestly defending himself against possessing the qualities I had attributed to him, however estimable they might be.

I did not regard myself as beaten. I replied that nature never worked without an object; that she had evidently formed him for certain missions, and that if he was abstemious it was by self-constraint. I, however, had no right to challenge his word.

The correspondence ended here; but, shortly after, all Paris was informed by the morning papers of the memorable pugilistic encounter between the minister and his cook. The battle was long disputed, and his Excellency had not always the best of it. Now, if after such an adventure, the cook was not dismissed (and he was not), I think I may draw the conclusion that the duke was absolutely dominated by the talents of that artiste, and that he despaired of finding another one who could flatter his taste so agreeably, otherwise he never could have overcome the very natural repugnance he must have felt at having so bellicose a servant.

As I was writing the above lines, on a fine winters evening, M. Cartier, ex-premier violon of the opera, entered my room, and sat down by the fire. Being full of my subject, I looked at him with attention. " My dear professor!" I exclaimed, " how comes it you are not a gourmand? You possess all the features of one." " I was once," he replied, " but I am obliged to abstain;" and he gave a deep sigh, almost a groan, worthy of one of Sir Walter Scotts heroes.

But if there are gourmands by predestination, there are gourmands by profession. I will point out four great classes: financiers, doctors, literary men, and dandvots.

Financiers are the heroes of good cheer. Hero is the word, for they do battle; and the aristocracy would have crushed the financiers under the weight of their titles and quarterings, if the latter had not brought into the field against them sumptuous tables and their strong boxes. Cooks fought genealogists; and although dukes did not wait till they had left the room to sneer at their Amphitryon, nevertheless, they came, and, by their presence, admitted their defeat.

Moreover, all those who make large fortunes easily, are almost compelled to become gourmands.

Inequality of conditions implies inequality of riches, but inequality of riches does not imply inequality of wants; and the man who could afford every day to pay for a dinner that would feed a hundred, is often satisfied himself with the wing of a fowl. Art, therefore, must be had recourse to, to reanimate that shadow of appetite by dishes that encourage it without hurt, and flatter it without stifling it. It was thus that Mondor became a gourmand, and that from all quarters gourmands assembled round him.

It is thus that in every cookery-book we are sure to find one or more dishes styled a lafinan-ciere. And it is a known fact that it was not the king, but the fermiers-generaux, who formerly ate the first dish of green peas, which always cost 800 francs.

Matters have not changed in our times; the tables of our financiers continue to offer the best that nature can produce, hot-houses bring forth, or art accomplish; and the most noted men of the day do not disdain a seat at their banquets.

Causes of another nature, though not less powerful, act upon the medical profession; they are gourmands by seduction, and they must be men of bronze to resist the temptations offered them.

The " dear doctors " axe all the better welcome, as health, which is under their care, is the most precious of all goods; thus they become " spoiled children " in every sense of the word.

Always anxiously expected, they are eagerly welcomed; they are treated like turtle-doves; they gradually like it; in six months it becomes a habit, and they become gourmands past redemption.

One day I hazarded to express this at a dinnerparty, I myself figuring as the ninth, Dr. Corvisart in the chair. This was in 1806.

"You are," I exclaimed, in the inspired tones of a Puritan preacher, " you are the last remnant of a corporation which once covered the whole of France. Alas! its members are now annihilated or dispersed; no more fei miers-ginereaux, no more abbes, no more knights, no monks of the white robe; the whole body of good taste rests now with you. Maintain with dignity so great a responsibility, even should you share the fate of the 300 Spartans at the pass of Thermopylae!"

I said, and there was not one dissentient voice; we acted accordingly, and the truth remains.

I made an observation at this dinner which is worthy of record.

Dr. Corvisart, who, when he chose, could make himself most agreeable, drank nothing but iced champagne; thus, from the very commencement of the dinner, he was noisy, witty, and full of anecdotes, whilst the others were plying knife and fork. At dessert, on the contrary, when conversation was just beginning to get lively, he became serious, taciturn, almost morose.

From that observation, and others of a similar nature, I have come to this conclusion: I " Champagne, which is exhilarating in its first effect (ab initio), is stupifying in its consequences (i/n, recessu), which, moreover, is a noted effect of the acid-carbonic gas which it contains.

Before leaving the subject of medical men, I have a crow to pluck with them. I do not wish to die without reproaching them with the extreme severity they sometimes exercise towards their patients. As soon as a poor fellow falls into their clutches, he is at once forbidden everything that is agreeable. I protest against the majority of those interdictions as useless.

I say useless, because a sick man never longs for anything likely to hurt him.

A clever doctor should never lose sight of the natural tendency of our inclinations, nor forget that if painful sensations are baneful from their very nature, agreeable ones are conducive to health. I have seen a glass of wine, a cup of coffee, or a few drops of liqueur, revive a desponding invalid.

Moreover, they must be well aware that their severe prescriptions are generally eluded by the sick man; his friends find plenty of excuses for humouring him, and he dies neither sooner nor later.

I give my opinion with the more confidence, as it is supported by numerous facts, and the most flourishing practitioners approve the system.

The Chanoine Kollet, who died some fifty years since, was a clergyman, of the old school, and a hard drinker, as was customary in his day; he fell sick, and the first edict of his physician was to prohibit him from tasting wiite. Nevertheless, at his next visit the doctor found his patient in bed, and at the side of it a small table covered with a snow-white cloth, a goodly-looking bottle and glass, and a napkin to wipe his lips. At this sight he flew into a great rage, when the unfortunate man in a lamentable voice exclaimed; " Ah! doctor, when you forbade me to taste wine, you did not prohibit the pleasure of beholding the bottle."

The physician who attended M. de Montlusin, of Pont-de-Veyle, was still more cruel, for not only did he prohibit the use of wine to his patient, but prescribed him large doses of cold water.

As soon as he had left, Madame de Montlusin, eager to obey the doctors orders and to contribute to the restoration of her husband to health, offered him a large tumbler of water pure as crystal.

The invalid took it with docility and began to drink it with resignation; but he stopped short after the first mouthful, and returning the glass to his wife; " Take it, my dear, (he said), and keep it for another time; I always heard we should not trifle with remedies."

In the empire of Gastronomy, the quartier of literary men is close to that of the medical fraternity.

In the reign of Louis XIV. literary men were drunkards; they followed the fashion, and the memoirs of that day are quite edifying on the subject. Now they are gourmands, it is a step in the right direction.

I am far from sharing the opinion of the Cynic Geoffroy, that modern productions are so wanting in force, because the writers drink nothing but eau sucrie. On the contrary, I believe he is doubly wrong, both as regards the fact and the consequence.

Men of letters are invited because of the esteem their talents are held in, because their conversation has, generally speaking, something piquant in it, and also because it has latterly become a custom that every dinner should have its " man of letters."

These gentlemen generally arrive late, and are all the better received because they are expected; they are made most of to induce them to come again; they are given all sorts of delicacies that they may shine, and as they find all this very natural, they get accustomed to it, become, are, and remain gourmands.

Matters even went so far as to cause a little scandal. Slanderous tongues have whispered that at certain breakfasts certain litterateurs have been bribed; that situations have issued forth from certain pates, and that the temple of Immortality has been opened with a fork. But they are evil tongues, and I only make this passing allusion to show that I am up in my subject.

Finally, many disciples of "gourmandise" are to be found amongst the divots.

All men who enter a profession, endeavour to walk along the path they have chosen, as pleasantly as possible, and this is applicable to the church as well as to any other. The man who sleeps on the hard rock and does penance, is an exception.

Now there are some things strictly forbidden, as balls, theatres, gambling, and other amusements; whilst they are anathematised as well as those who patronise them, good-living steps in quietly with a jolly rubicund clerical countenance.

By divine right, man is the king of nature, and all that the earth produces was created for his use. It is for him the quail gets plump and fat, it is for him the Mocca exhales its fine iroma, it is for him that sugar was made favourable to health.

Why, then, should the good things offered to us by Providence be neglected, especially if we look upon them as perishable things: more especially, if they awaken our gratitude towards the Creator of all things.

No less cogent reasons come to the support of the above. Can we receive too hospitably those who guide us in the right path? Ought we not to invite often, and be kind to those whose object is so praiseworthy?

Sometimes the gifts of Comus drop in quite unsought for; a souvenir from a college chum, a gift from an old friend, a peace offering from a penitent. How refuse to accept such offerings? It is sheer necessity.

Moreover, it has always been so. Monasteries have ever been depots of rare delicacies, and this is why many amateurs regret their loss.

The best liqueurs of France were made at the monastery of the Visitandines; angelica (preserve) was invented at Niort; the sisters of Chateau-Thierry invented the pains de fleur tforange; the Ursulines of Belley had a receipt for pickled walnuts, unrivalled.

Many monastic orders, especially that of St. Bernard, were renowned for their good cheer. The cooks of the clergy enlarged the circle of culinary art. When M. de Pressigni, archbishop of Be-sanpon, returned from the Conclave which had elected Pius VI., he said the best dinner he had at Eome, was at the table of the head of the Ca-pucins.

THE INFLUENCE OF GOOD LIVING ON CONJUGAL HAPPINESS.

Finally, the love of good living, when shared, has a marked influence on conjugal happiness. Husband and wife, if both love good cheer, will at all events meet once a day, should they even have separate apartments, and pass a pleasant hour at table: they can discuss not only what they are eating, but what they have eaten, and what they intend to eat; they can talk of new dishes, modern innovations, and interchange that sort of chit-chat which is so charming.

Music has doubtless its charms for those who love it; but it requires attention, and is a labour. Moreover, a man may have a cold, the music-book may be mislaid, the lady have the migraine; –there is a hitch.

A want which is shared, on the contrary, calls a married couple to table, both actuated by the same inclination; they pay each other those little delicate attentions which betray a wish to oblige; and the manner in which the daily repasts are partaken of has a great influence upon the happiness of life.

Fielding has ably developed this truth in one of his novels.

Honour, then, to gourmandise, such as we present it to our readers, so long as it does not take away man from his occupations or his duties! The orgies of Sardanapalus do not make us despise all womankind, nor do the excesses of Vitellius make us turn our back upon a well-organised banquet. When it degenerates into gluttony, it loses its name, its charms, and falls into the hands of the moralist, who will censure it, or of the doctor, who will cure it with medicines.

A DAT WITH THE MONKS OF ST. BERNARD.

It was in the year 1782. It was about one oclock A. m.; it was a beautiful summer night; a party of young men, myself amongst the number, formed a cavalcade, and after first serenading the fair ladies in whom we felt an interest, we started on our excursion.

We left Belley and took the road towards St. Sulpice, a monastery belonging to the order of St. Bernard, situated on one of the highest mountains of the district, at least 5000 feet above the level of the sea. I was at that time the leader of a band of amateur musicians, all jolly fellows, and endowed with all the gifts of youth and health. At a dinner one day, the Abbe of St. Sulpice took me aside into a window recess, and said, "My dear Sir, if you would come with your friends and give us a little music on the fete-day of our saint, it would be to the glory of the saint, it would delight our neighbours, and you would be the first sons of Orpheus who have penetrated into our elevated regions."

I did not let him repeat the request, but at once accepted:

"Annuit, et totum nutu tremefecit Olympum."

We took all our precautions beforehand, and left at the early hour already mentioned, because we had four leagues to travel over roads steep enough to try the boldest traveller.

The monastery was built in a valley shut in on the west side by the summit of the mountain, and on the east by a less elevated cone. The peak on the west side was crowned by a forest of fir-trees, of which 37,000 were blown down by one storm. The valley itself consisted of pasture land and fields hedged in in the English style. We reached the monastery at daybreak, and were received by the bursar, a monk with a massive head and a nose like an obelisk.

"Gentlemen," said the worthy father, " you are welcome; it will gladden the heart of our reverend abbot when he knows you have arrived: he is still in bed, being much fatigued from exertion yesterday; but come with me, and you will see that we expected you."

He led the way, and we followed him, guessing rightly he was taking us to the refectory. There all our senses were aroused at the sight of a most seductive breakfast, truly classic. In the centre of the large table rose a pasty as large as a church, flanked on one side by a cold quarter of veal, on the south by an enormous ham, on the east by a huge pile of butter, and on the west by a bushtl of artichokes a la poivrade.

Fruit of every description, plates, napkins, knives, and silver spoons and forks in baskets were spread over the table, and at the end of the hall were a number of lay servants ready to wait upon us, though rather astonished at such an early gathering.

la one corner of the refectory more than one hundred bottles were placed under a rippling jet of pure water from the rock, murmuring, as it were, Evoe Bacche; and if the aroma of Mocca did not greet our nostrils, it was because in those heroic days coffee was not taken so early.

The reverend bursar for some time enjoyed our astonishment, and then addressed us in the following speech, which, in our wisdom, we settled he had prepared beforehand.

"Gentlemen," he said, "I wish I could keep you company; but I have not yet heard matins, and this is a great day. I might invite you to eat, but your years, your ride, and the mountain air will do that for you. Accept heartily what we heartily offer: I leave you to say my matins."

He left us, and we set too with all the vigour of hungry youth. But the efforts of us poor children of Adam were of no avail against a repast seemingly prepared for the children of Sirius. We left but a small mark of our attack. We were then shown to the dormitory, where I was soon snug in a good bed, like the hero of Eocroy, determined to sleep till the battle trumpet sounded.

I was awakened by a robust friar, who nearly pulled my arms out of their sockets, and who informed me that Mass was about to be performed. I hastened to the chapel, where I found every one at his post.

We executed a symphony, an anthem, and other religious pieces, finishing with a quatuor of wind instruments, and, with all due modesty be it said, I think we managed pretty well.

Praises were showered upon us, and, after having received the thanks of the abbot, we sat down to dinner.

Dinner was served in the style of the fifteenth century; few side dishes, few superfluities, but an excellent choice of meat, simple, substantial ragouts, all well cooked, and vegetables of a flavour unknown to the lowlands.

Abundance seemed the order of the day. At the second course there were no less than fourteen different dishes of roast.

The dessert was the more remarkable, as it consisted of fruits not to be found at such an elevation; the valleys at the foot of the mountains had been placed under contribution for the occasion.

Liqueurs were handed round, but the coffee deserves special mention. It was clear, perfumed, and beautifully hot. It was not served up in those degenerated vases called cups on the banks of the Seine, but in deep bowls, out of which the thick lips of the monks sucked it in with a loud note of satisfaction.

After dinner we attended vespers, and between the psalms we performed some sacred music I had composed expressly for the occasion.

The days ceremonials being over, the neighbours began to leave; others played games in the open air. I preferred a stroll, and, with a few others, wandered about inhaling the pure air of these elevated regions, which is so refreshing to the mind, and disposes the imagination to meditation and romance.

It was late when we returned. The worthy Superior came to wish us good-night; "I am going," he said to me, " to my own apartments, and will leave you to yourselves for the rest of the evening; not because I think my presence would be a restraint upon my worthy brethren, but because I wish them to know they are at perfect liberty. It is not every day St. Bernard. Tomorrow we resume our usual daily avocations, eras iterabimus cequor."

" I have constantly " (says Savarin) " experienced this effect under similar circumstances, and I am inclined to believe that the lightness of the air in the mountains allow certain cerebral powers to act which its heaviness oppresses in the plains."

As soon as the Superior had left, the monks became more lively, and a good deal of good-humoured joking went on.

At nine oclock supper was served,–a careful, delicate repast, three centuries removed from the dinner. We all ate heartily; songs were sung, and one of the worthy fathers spouted some verses of his own composition, which were not bad for a monk.

Towards the close of the evening, a voice exclaimed, "Father cellarer, where is your dish? " " All right," replied the venerable monk, "I am not cellarer for nothing!"

He left the refectory, and soon after returned, followed by three servants, one bearing plates of excellent buttered toast, and the others with a table and a huge bowl of burning spirits and sugar equivalent to punch, the concoction of which was not then universally known.

We did ample honour to the cellarer. As the clock of the monastery struck midnight, each re tired to his apartment to enjoy the sweets of slumber, to which the days labours had given inclination and a claim.

The father cellarer mentioned above, having grown old, and being told that a new Superior was coming from Paris, reputed a stern man, "I am easy about it," he said; " let him be as bad as he can be, he can never have the heart to deprive an old man of his seat iu the chimney-corner, or to take the key of the cellar from him."

Let it be observed that good cheer is by no means detrimental to health; and, taking everything into equal consideration, your good eater lives the longest. This has been proved statistically in a very able article read at the Academy of Sciences by Dr. Villermet. He has compared the different states of society where men eat well with those where they are badly fed. He has even compared various districts of Paris, and has proved, for instance, a great difference of mortality between the Faubourg St. Marceau and the Chaussee dantin. It must not be supposed that a high-feeder never falls ill. But he has more vitality in him, all parts of his system are better nourished, nature has more resources, and the body has incomparably more power to resist destruction,,

This physiological truth is supported by history, which informs us that every time imperious circumstances, as war, sieges, sudden changes in the seasons, have diminished the means of food, that state of distress has always been accompanied by contagious diseases and a great increase of mortality.

M. du Belloy, Archbishop of Paris, who lived nearly a century, had a great appetite; he loved good cheer; I have often seen his patriarchal countenance beam at the sight of some favourite dish. On every occasion Napoleon showed him the most marked deference and respect.

CHAP, XI.
PROUVETTES GASTRONOMIQUES.

Up to the present chapter, these pages, with a few exceptions, have been nothing more than a free translation of Savarins Physiologie du Gout. The recent movement in the "Art of Giving Dinners," taken up by the leading journal and immediately responded to by hundreds of " dinner-givers" (Amphitryons is the classical term) of both sexes, induced us to translate Savarin. As is correctly observed by an elegant writer in the Quarterly Eeview, " there exists nothing in English at all comparable to it." The same writer observes: " The history of gastronomy is that of manners, if not of morals; and the learned are aware that its literature is both instructive and amusing, for it is replete with curious traits of character and comparative views of society at different periods, as well as with striking anecdotes of remarkable men and women, whose destinies have been strangely influenced by their epicurean tastes and habits. Let it, moreover, be remembered, that a tone of mock seriousness or careless gaiety does not necessarily imply the absence of sound reflection. The laughing philosopher may prove better worth attention than the solemn pedant."

July, 1835.

As a man enters a church in a careless mood, and is suddenly struck by some observations from the preacher, and becomes an attentive listener, so will many a man who takes up this book read it through, and put it down with the conviction that convivial intercourse is capable of much higher refinement than is usually given to it.

Under the head of " tprouvettes gastrono-miques" Savarin gives the menu for a dinner suited to various degrees of fortune.

By eprouvettes gastronomiques we mean (says Savarin) dishes of such recognised flavour and of such indisputable excellence, that their apparition alone ought, in a well-organised man, to move all his faculties of taste; so that those who, on such an occasion, evince no spark of desire, no radiance of ecstasy, ought to be justly noted as unworthy of the honours of the sitting and of the pleasures attached thereto.

The system of eprouvettes, duly examined and deliberated in full council, has been inscribed in the "golden book" in a tongue that changes bot:–

"Utcumque ferculum, eximii et bend noti saporis, appositum fuerit, fiat autopsia con-vivce, et nisi fades ejus ac oculi vertantur ad extasim, notetur ut indiynus"

In other words:–" Whenever a dish of distinguished flavour or renown is served up, scan attentively the countenance of every guest, and note down as unworthy all those whose countenances do not beam with delight."

The power of Eprouvettes is relative, and must be suited to the habits and capacities of every class of society. All circumstances considered, an eprouvette must be calculated to create admiration and surprise. It is a dynamometer, which increases as we approach the higher zones of society. Thus, an eprouvette (in other words, a dinner),, given by a shopkeeper in the Strand, would not. tell upon a clerk in a first-rate concern; whilst upon a select few assembled at the table of a minister or a financier, it would not even be thought of.

This gives us a maxim at once:–

"Let your dinner be according to the guests you invite."

As the reader progresses through these pages, many other truths will force themselves upon his mind. Let him turn occasionally to the aphorisms in Chapter I.; for instance, aphorisms xvi. and xvii., on Punctuality; and xviii., xix., and xx. Gradually we shall arrive at grand conclusions.

For a fortune of about 2001. a year, Savarin gives the following as a good dinner:—

A roast fillet of veal, larded, with gravy.
A farmyard turkey, stuffed with chesnuts.
Stewed pigeons.

A dish of stewed cabbage (Saverkrauf), ornamented with sausages, and crowned by a fine piece of bacon. (Eufs a la neige.

II.

For a fortune of 600?. per annum:-
A fillet of beef piqui, roasted, with gravy.
A quarter of chevreuil (venison), sauce hackee aux cornichons.
A turbot, au nature!.
A gigot of mutton, a la proven ale.
A dindon trvffe.
Early green peas.
Pre-sale, equal to our Dartmoor or Welsh mutton.
For a fortune of 12001. per annum and upwards:
A carp, a la Chambord.
A river pike, stuffed and smothered in a cream of prawns, secundum artem.
A capon of seven pounds, crammed with Perigord truffles.
A large Strasbourg pate de foie-gras.
Truffled quails on toast, au basilic.
A pheasant, a la sainte alliance.
100 asparagus (early), sauce a fomazome.
A dish of ortolans, a la provenfale.
A pyramid of meringues, a la vanille and a la rose.

The latter is not a bad dinner. It is curious that Savarin makes no mention of soup or dessert in these eprouvettes, probably taking them as a matter of course. Moreover, the dishes enumerated must necessarily vary according to the season of the year. As regards fish, in his day, sea-fish was not so easily to be had in Paris. Eailways considerably modify his carte. Instead of the pike, for instance, red mullets, or a John a Dory, or soles a la Hol-landaise.

In a word, then, variety, and of the best, is another maxim. It also implies a good cook. There is another point worthy of observation: truffles. They are sorely wanting at our English dinner-tables. Very, in Eegent Street, gives a very good capilotade de faisan aux truffes, for which dish he charges six shillings, and it gives some idea of the great addition truffles, are to the table. In Sardinia and Lombardy, truffles are served up alone, fried in butter with cut lemons to squeeze over them. They are delicious.

Another, and what has often struck us as a radical evil in English dinners, is that so many dishes are placed upon the table at once. Unless our dishes are i la Russe, with spirits of wine burning under each, all the entrees are generally cold when handed to you. Moreover, nothing should be carved at table. The host gets "red in the face from exertion, and cannot possibly "attend to the lady he has taken down to dinner; whilst the unfortunate man who has had the honour of taking down the lady of the house is like a culprit going to execution. He has a presentiment going downstairs that he will have to carve two fowls smothered in white sauce; he is seldom deceived, and gets no dinner till the third course. We are here talking of dinners in town, not family dinners. God forbid that our good old English custom should ever go out, or the head of the family be found sitting at home with only a table-cloth before him.

Dinners are well given in the higher circles in Germany.

Every guest (we are not speaking of public dinners) has a sort of proces verbal of the menu placed by the side of his plate. He knows then how to regulate his appetite. The table has nothing on it but epergnes full of the choicest flowers, and, as many of the ladies carry bouquets, the room is agreeably perfumed. The dishes are handed round by servants, and vanish. Your glass is never left empty by the attentive butler, who softly asks you which wine you prefer. Conversation is not interrupted. As soon as dessert is over, all rise together, the doors of the drawing-room are thrown open, and excellent coffee and liqueurs handed round. The guest is now a free man; the lady of the house is probably going to the opera. If you are a favourite, she may intimate that she expects you to look in.

The men have dined well and lightly, and are not heavy with wine. All is merry as a church-bell.

Another maxim: Do not let the men sit so long as is now the custom.

Often have we broken through the magic circle of petticoats in the drawing-room, and always been received with pleasure for doing so.

To turn from these (if we may so term them) outside observations, let us come again to the more substantial.

The letters which have recently appeared in the London journals, from all parts of England, have struck a key-note which will echo for some time to come. They threatened for a moment to throw the Eeform Bill of Mr. Bright into the shade.

Another point worthy of observation is this:

All ladies like rissoles, whether of lobster or chicken matters not.

Curry is too hot for them; they will eat sweetbread, but rissoles are No. 1. A. They will also partake of oyster-pates.

It is curious that Savarin does not mention Charlottes-Russes,

All ladies like ice, particularly a la vanille, and dethoif object (though they often refuse it) to a glass of Maraschino after it.

Weteme it a mistake to have game and pudding brought up together. How can a gentle girl eat sweets, when the man next to her is eating a piece of woodcock so high that she nearly faints?

After this little digression, let us return once more to Savarin.

For an eprouvette to be certain in producing

the desired effect, it must necessarily be, comparatively, on a large scale; experience, founded on the knowledge of the human species, has taught us that the most rare delicacy loses. its influence when not in exuberant proportion; the first movement of pleasure amongst the guests is justly checked by the fear that they will be stingily served, or have to decline out of politeness.

We have often witnessed the effect of " eprou-vettes gastronomiques." I will mention one: I was present at a dinner of gourmands of the fourth category (clericals).–My friend J–E–and myself the only profane.

After an excellent first course, a huge truffled fowl was brought up, and a Gibraltar-looking monster Strasbourg pate de foie-gras.

This apparition produced a marked effect upon the assembly like the " silent laugh" of Cooper, difficult to describe.

Conversation dropped as if by tacit consent from the fulness of the heart; and as each guests plate was filled, I saw the eagerness of desire, the ecstasy of enjoyment, and, ultimately, the perfect repose of bliss on every countenance.

CHAP. XII.

THE PLEASURES OF THE TABLE.

Man is incontestably the most sensitive being that inhabits our globe, the one which undergoes the most suffering.

Nature in the first instance condemned him to pain by the nudity of his skin, by the formation of his feetj and by the instinct of war and des-tructiveness which accompanies the human species wherever it has been found.

Animals have not this curse upon them; and with the exception of a few battles on the score of jealousy, suffering, in the state of nature, would be almost unknown to most species; whilst man who can only experience pleasure in a passing manner, by a restricted number of organs, is always open, in every part of his body, to the risk of excruciating pain.

This decree of destiny has been aggravated in its execution by a host of ills ema-nating from the habits of social life; so that the most lively and con tinuous pleasure we can imagine cannot, either in intensity or duration, compensate us for the atrocious pain which accompanies certain ills, as gout, tooth-ache, rheumatism, andc.

It is this practical fear of pain which makes man, without his being aware of it, throw himself bodily into the opposite camp, and he gives himself up to the small number of pleasures nature has allotted to him.

It is from the same reason that he increases them, draws them out, shapes them, fi-nally, worships them. For many centuries during the reign of idolatry all the secondary divinities represented the pleasures presided over by the superior gods.

The severity of the Christian religion has destroyed all those patrons. Bacchus, Cupid, Comus, Diana, are nothing more than poetical souvenirs; but the thing subsists; and under the most serious of all religions we carouse at marriages, baptisms, and even at funerals.

Eepasts, in the sense which we give to the word, commenced with the second era of the human race, that is to say, when it ceased to live upon fruits. The preparation and distribution of food rendered a meeting of the family necessary; the fathers distributed to their children the pro duce of their chase, and, in their turn, adult children rendered the same service to their parents.

Those meetings, limited at first to blood relations, extended gradually to friends and neighbours.

At a later period, as the human race increased in number, the weary traveller would find a seat at those primitive repasts, and relate the sights he had seen in foreign lands.

Thus was hospitality born with rights held sacred by every nation; for no matter how ferocious the race, it held it a sacred duty to respect the life of the man who had eaten its bread and salt.

It is during repasts that language must have been improved, because men continually met, and confidence and conversation was the result.

Such must have been, from the nature of things, the elements of " the pleasures of the table," which is perfectly distinct, let it be understood, from the " pleasure of eating," which is its necessary antecedent.

The pleasure of eating is the actual and direct sensation of a want which is satisfied.

We share the pleasure of eating in common with all animals; it simply implies hunger and wherewithal to satisfy it.

The pleasures of the table are peculiar to the human race. It premises preparation beforehand for the repast, the locality, and the selection of guests.

The pleasure of eating requires, if not hunger, at least, appetite; the pleasures of the table are, generally, independent of both.

Both states may always be observed at our banquets.

At the first course men eat eagerly, without speaking or paying attention to what may be said; and, whatever may be our rank in society, we forget everything to set to work like the others. But when our cravings begin to feel satisfied, reflection steps in, conversation opens, a new order of things commences, and the man who up to this point was only an eater, becomes a more or less agreeable companion, according to the means given him by the master of all things.

The pleasures of the table do not consist in transports of delight or ecstasies; but they gain in duration what they lose in intensity, and have the peculiar privilege of disposing us to all others, or of consoling us for their loss.

And, in sooth, after a good dinner, soul and body feel happy and comfortable.

Physically, whilst the brain is lighter, the countenance brightens, the colour rises, the eyes sparkle, a warm heat runs through our veins. Morally, the intellect is brighter, the imagination warms, and wit and humour follow.

Moreover, we often find assembled round the same table, all the modifications which extreme sociability has introduced amongst us. Love, friendship, business, speculation, power, solicitation, protection, ambition, intrigue; hence conviviality concerns everything; hence it produces fruits of every flavour.

The immediate consequence of these antecedents is, that every branch of human industry exerts itself to add to and increase the intensity of the pleasures of the table.

The goblet and jugs were ornamented with flowers, and the guests crowned with wreaths; banquets were held in the open air, in gardens, surrounded by all the beauties of nature.

To the pleasures of the table were added the charms of music and the sound of instruments.

At times, dancers and comic actors were intro duced to occupy the eye without interference with the taste; the most exquisite perfumes exhaled their odour around; a further step was taken, and the most beautiful women were engaged to wait upon the guests.

Vide Centuras picture: La decadence liomaine. Boccacios Decamerone is descriptive of another epoch of this refined epicurism.

Volumes might be written on this subject, but Greek and Eoman authors are at hand to corroborate what I advance.

In the 18th and 19th centuries, we have, more or less, according to circumstances, adopted these various means of gratifying the senses, and. we have, moreover, added what new discoveries have revealed to us.

However, these accessories are not indispensable to constitute the pleasures of a table. Four conditions suffice, viz.: good cheer, good wine, amiable companions, and time sufficient.

Thus have I often wished for that frugal repast which Horace destined for his neighbour, or to some unexpected guest constrained to find shelter under his roof; namely, a good fowl, a piece of fat venison, and for dessert, grapes, figs, and nuts. Add to this, wine of the vintage of the Consul Manlius (nata mecum consule Manlio), and the conversation of that voluptuous poet, and I flatter myself I should have supped well.

"At mihi cum longnm post tcmpus venerat hosprs,
Sive operum vacuo, longum conviva per imbrem
Vicinas, ben erat, non piscibus urbe petitis,
Sed pallo atque luwlo, turn pcnsilis uva secundas
Et nux ornabat mensas, cum duplicc fica."

HOW TO GIVE A DINNEB.

A dinner, no matter how recherche, how sumptuous, will never go off well if the wine is bad; the guests not suited to each other, the faces dull, and the dinner eaten hastily.

But some impatient reader will exclaim, How can we, manage to unite all these conditions which enhance, in a supreme degree, the pleasures of the dinner-table?

I will reply to this question, so listen attentively, gentle reader. It is Gasterea, the prettiest of the muses, who inspires me; I will be clearer than an oracle, and my precepts will live for centuries.

Let the number of your guests never exceed twelve, so that the conversation may constantly remain general.

Let them be so collected that their occupations are different, their tastes similar, and with such points of contact, that it is not necessary to go through the odious form of introduction.

Let your dining-room be brilliantly lighted, your cloth perfectly clean, and the temperature of the room from 13 to 16 Reaumur. "Let the men be clever without presumption, the women amiable without conceit.

Let your dishes be limited in number, but each excellent, and your wines first-rate. Let the former vary from the most substantial to the most light; and for the second, from the strongest to the most perfumed.

Let everything be served quietly, without hurry or bustle; dinner being the last business of the day. Let your guests look upon themselves as travellers who have arrived at the end of their journey.

Let the coffee be very hot, and the liqueurs first quality.

Let your drawing-room be spacious enough to allow a game to be played, if desired, without interfering with those addicted to chatting.

Let the guests be retained by the pleasant company, and cheered with the hope that, before the evening is over, there is something good still in store for them.

Let the tea not be too strong; the hot toast well buttered; and the punch carefully mixed.

Let no one leave before eleven, but let every one be in bed by midnight.

I have said that the pleasures of the table were susceptible of long duration; I will prove it by a little anecdote, true and circumstantial, of the longest repast I ever made in my life. It is a little bon-bon I slip into the readers mouth for having read me attentively so far.

A family, relations of mine, lived in the Eue du Bac, consisting of a doctor, aged seventy-eight, a captain, seventy-six, and their sister Jeannette, seventy-four. I sometimes paid them a visit, and was always well received.

"Parbleu!" said Dr. Dubois to me one day, rising on his toes to reach my shoulder, " you have long been praising your fondues (eggs beaten up with cheese) to us, making our mouths water; it is time to put an end to it. We will come and breakfast with you some day, the captain and I, and see what they are like."

"Willingly," I replied, "and you shall have one in all its glory, for I shall make it myself. Your proposal has given me great pleasure. I expect you to-morrow at ten–military punctuality." Punctual to the hour came my two old friends, still hale and hearty, clean shaven and combed.

They smiled with pleasure when they saw the table laid for three, and at each plate two dozen oysters, with a bright golden lemon.

At each end of the table stood a bottle of Sau-terne, carefully wiped, all, except the cork, which indicated its quality in an unmistakable manner.

Alas! these oyster luncheons have gradually fallen off; they disappeared with the abbes, who always managed a gross, and the chevaliers, who never stopped. I regret them; but, philosophically, if time modifies governments, what right has it not over simple customs?

After the oysters, which were found fresh, we had some roasted kidneys, some foie-gras aux truffes, and finally the fondue.

The elements were collected in a pan, which was placed upon the table over a burner of spirits of wine. I functioned on the field of battle, and my cousins did not lose one of my movements. They were loud in their praises of the preparation, and asked for the recipe. I told them, moreover, two anecdotes, which the reader will find further on.

After the fondue we had fruit and preserves, a cup of real mocca a la Dubelloy, and two liqueurs, the first a spirit to settle down, the second oil to soften.

After breakfast I proposed a little exercise, and offered to show them over my house, which is far from being elegant, but is commodious and comfortable, the ceilings and gildings dating from the reign of Louis XV.

I showed them the original cast of my pretty cousin Madame Eecamier, by Chinard, and her miniature portrait, by Augustin; they were so charmed that the doctor kissed the portrait, whilst the captain took a similar liberty with the bust, for which I beat him; for if all the admirers of the original took a similar liberty, it would soon share the fate of the big toe of the statue of St. Peter at Eome, which pilgrims have considerably reduced by kissing.

I then showed them casts of some of the best antiques, some pictures, not without their merit, my guns, my musical instruments, and a few rare editions of French and foreign works. I showed them over my kitchen, explained to them my fuel economiser, my roasting oven and turn-spit with clock, steam valve, all of which they examined most minutely.

As we returned to the drawing-room it struck two oclock. " Peste!" exclaimed the doctor," it is dinner time, and sister Jeannette is waiting for us. We must go. I am not very hungry, but I should like my soup. It is an old habit, and if I omit it I exclaim, like Titus, diem perdidi!" "My dear doctor," I rejoined, " why go so far for what you have close at hand? I will send a messenger to your sister to tell her you stop to dinner with me. You must not be over particular, as it will not have the merit of a got up impromptu. 1

After an ocular consultation between the two brothers, the offer was accepted. I sent off a messenger to the Faubourg St. Germain, gave some instructions to my chef-de-cuisine, and in a very short time, what with his own resources and restaurateurs in the vicinity, he dished us up a very nice little dinner.

It was a great satisfaction to me to behold the sangfroid and aplomb with which my two friends sat down, drew their chairs close to the table, spread their napkins, and prepared for action.

They had two "surprises" of which I myself had not thought; I gave them grated parmesan with their soup, and a glass of Madeira sec after it. Both were novelties introduced a short time previously by Prince Talleyrand.

Dinner was done ample justice to, and my two guests made themselves most agreeable. After dinner I proposed a game of piquet, but they preferred the far niente, and we drew round the fire. Despite the pleasures of the far niente, I have always entertained the opinion that conversation runs smoother when some little occupation goes on, so I ordered tea.

Tea was a novelty for Frenchmen of the old school, but they drank two or three cups with the more relish, as hitherto they had looked upon it as a medicine. A long experience has taught me that complacency follows complacency. Therefore, almost in an imperative tone, I proposed to wind up with a bowl of punch.

"But you will kill us!" shouted the doctor, "You will make us drunk!" exclaimed the captain. I replied by calling loudly for lemons, sugar, and rum.

I mixed the punch; meantime delicate slices of thin toast, well buttered and salted, were under preparation. This time I met opposition; but as I knew the attractions of this simple preparation, I replied that I only hoped they had made enough for iis. Shortly afterwards the captain was despatching the last slice, and I saw a glance at the empty dish which made me order up some more.

Time was getting on, and the clock on my mantelpiece struck eight. " We must go now," said my guests, " and have a bit of salad with our sister, who has not seen us all day." I made no objection, and saw them safely to their carriage. During the whole time they were with me not one of us felt the slightest ennui. The doctor was full of anecdotes, and the captain had spent many years in Italy in the army, and on a mission to the Court of Parma, and so our conversation never lagged.

On the morrow I received a note to inform me that far from having suffered from the little excess of the evening before, they had slept like tops, and were quite ready to try me again.

HOW TO MAKE A "FONDUE."

Take the same number of eggs as of the guests you invite.

Take then a piece of good fromage de Gruyere weighing about one third, and a piece of butter one sixth of this weight.

Break and beat up your eggs well in a saucepan; then add your cheese and butter grated.

Put your saucepan on the fire and stir it with a wooden spoon until the substance is thick and soft; put in a little salt, according to the age of the cheese, and a good sprinkling of pepper, which is one of the positive characteristics of this ancient dish; serve up on a warm dish. Get some of your best wine from the cellar, which pass round briskly, and you will see wonders.

LA POULARDE DE BRESSE.

(A Caudle Lecture.)

These little dejeuners are nice little things, but they sometimes have the effect of upsetting the other arrangements of the day. I have the following little anecdote from Madame de Franval, who could not keep the secret.

It was early in January, 1825, a young married couple, Mme. and M. de Versy, were present at a dejeuner dhuitres –bien selle et bride; we know what that means. The party was a pleasant one, and ample justice done to the good fare. But when the dinner-hour came, though the young couple sat down to table, it was simply pro forma. Madame took a spoonful of potnge, and Monsieur drank a glass of wine-and-water; some friend dropped in, a rubber of whist was played, the; evening passed over, and the pair retired to rest.

About two oclock in the morning, M. de Versy awoke; he was uncomfortable; he yawned, and was so restless that his wife became anxious, and asked him if he was ill. " No, my dear," he said, " but I fancy I am hungry; and I was thinking of that poularde de Bresse, which looked so tempting, and which we did not touch at dinner." "Well, to tell the truth," replied Madame de Versy, " mon ami, I am every bit as hungry as you, and as you have mentioned the poulet, let us have it." "What folly! every one in the house is asleep, and we shall be laughed at to-morrow." " If everybody is asleep, then everybody shall get up, and we shall not be laughed at, as nobody will hear about it. Besides, one or both of us may die of hunger before to-morrow, and I for one do not intend to run the risk. I will ring for Justine."

So said, so done: the poor ladys maid was roused up, who, having eaten a good supper, slept like a young girl of nineteen without cares.

She entered yawning, with heavy eyes, to know what was wanted.

But the difficulty was not yet over. It was necessary to rouse the cook: the latter grumbled, growled, and was recalcitrant. However, she at last got up.

Meantime Madame de Versy had put on a dressing-gown and her husband made himself as comfortable as he could, whilst Justine had spread a napkin on the bed and brought the indispensable accessories to this improvise repast.

Everything thus prepared, the poularde was brought in, cut up and demolished without mercy. After this first exploit, the young couple ate a large pear between them, and some confiture cporange.

In the entractes they had nearly finished a bottle of vin-de-Grave, and had exclaimed more than once that they never enjoyed a repast so much.

The repast, like everything else in this world, terminated at last. Justine took away the fragments, and the conjugal curtains were drawn.

On the morrow, Madame de Versy told the whole story to her bosom friend, Madame de Franval; and it is to the indiscretion of the latter lady that the public is indebted for this little anecdote.

She never omitted to state, when she came to the end of her story, that Madame de Versy coughed twice, and positively blushed.

A PERSONAL ADVENTURE.

Savarin loved a good dinner. The smell of a roast pheasant or turkey acted upon him like the sound of the bugle on the war-horse, or the " full cry" on the hunter in the field. Though on a mission in which his head was at stake, he could not resist the temptation of stopping on the road to enjoy the good things which Providence threw in his way. He thus relates his adventure:—

Mounted on my good nag " La Joie "one day, I was riding through the laughing hills of the Jura, It was in the worst days of the Eevolution; I was on my way to Dole, to see the representative Prot, to obtain a " safe conduct," which might prevent me from being sent to prison, and from thence, probably, to the scaffold.

At about eleven oclock in the morning, I stopped at a small inn in the little village of Montsous-Vaudrey. I first saw that my nag had a good feed, and then made my way into the kitchen, when I was struck by a sight which would delight any traveller.

A spit was turning before a glowing fire, admirably furnished with quails–king-quails–fat and plump; the gravy from them was dropping on a fine piece of toast, which showed a knowing hand, whilst close by a leveret, already roasted, was keeping hot, the perfume of which tickled my nostrils

"Good!" I inwardly ejaculated; " Providence has not yet forsaken me. Let us cull this flower on the road; there is always time to die.r

Turning to the host, who, during this examination, was whistling, with his hands behind his back, walking up and down his kitchen with the strides of a giant, "My good man," I said, " what can you give me good for dinner? " " Nothing but good, Sir; good boiled beef, good potato soup, a good shoulder of mutton, and good beans."

At this unexpected reply, a shiver of disappointment ran through my frame; I never eat boiled beef (bauilli) of which soup has been made, it is the meat without its juice; potatoes and beans tend to promote corpulency; the mutton did not tickle my fancy.

The host kept throwing side glances at me, as if he guessed the cause of my abject looks. "And for whom do you reserve all this game?" I said, in an annoyed tone of voice. " Alas! Sir," he said, with a voice of commiseration, "I cannot dispose of it; it belongs to some gentlemen of the law, who have been down here for the last ten days to make an estimate for a rich lady in the neighbourhood. They finished their work yesterday, and are going to have a jollification to-day." " Sir," I said, after a few moments deliberation, " take my compliments to those gentlemen, and say that a gentleman solicits as a favour to be admitted to share their dinner, and will willingly pay his part of the expenses, and that he will feel deeply obliged to them."

My host went on the errand.

But shortly afterwards, a fat, jolly-looking little man entered the kitchen, displaced two or three things, took the cover off one of the stew-pans, and went out again.

"Good!" said I to myself," he has been sent to have a look at me." And hope rose within me, for experience had already taught me that my exterior was not repulsive.

My heart beat, nevertheless, as loud as that of a candidate when the votes are being counted, when the host returned and said, " the gentlemen were much flattered at my proposal, and only awaited me to sit down to dinner."

I left with a spring, received the most hearty welcome, and in a few minutes we were quite at home.

What a good dinner!!! I will not enter into details, but I must make honourable mention of a fricassee de poulet aux truffes, only to be had "en province" so good, that it would have brought Tithonus to life again. Of the roast I have already spoken; it was done to a turn, and the obstacles I had to overcome to partake of it heightened its flavour.

The dessert consisted of a creme a la vanille, cheese, and various sorts of fruits. We washed all these down, first, with a light wine, subsequently with Hermitage, afterwards with a soft and generous wine of a straw-colour. Excellent coffee and liqueurs of Verdun crowned the repast. Not only was the dinner good, but we were very merry.

After speaking cautiously of the events of the day, all sorts of anecdotes went the round.

Songs were sung, and I volunteered the following impromptu on the occasion:
Air.–Du marfchal-ferrant.
"Quil est doux pour les voyageurs
De trouver daimables buveurs!
Ccst une vraie beatitude.
Entoure daussi bons enfans,
   Ma foi! je passerai ceans,
Libre de toute inquietude,
   Quatre jours,
   Quinze jours,
   Trente jours,
   Une annue.
Et bcnirais ma destinee."

We had been four hours at table; a walk was proposed, and I was politely asked to join and return to supper. It was, however, time for me to be off. The sun, already sinking in the West, warned me that I had not much time to spare. They would not allow me to pay my share in the dinner, and all came to see me mount. We shook hands all round, and parted the best friends in the world.

On reaching M. Profs residence, I found that I had been informed against, and he received me with sinister looks. I do not believe he was a man cruel by nature; but he had little intellect, and did not know how to wield the fearful power placed in his hands; he was like a child armed with the club of Hercules.

I was better received by Madame Prot, having brought a letter from a friend. By good luck, the conversation turned upon music. As soon as she found I was an amateur she was delighted. I spent the evening with them. I sang, she sang, we sang. I knew all her favourite airs. On leaving, Madame Prot put out her hand, and said, "Citoyen, a man who like you cultivates the fine arts is incapable of betraying his country; I know you came here to ask a favour from my husband: it shall be granted, I promise you.

I kissed her hand respectfully, and on the morrow I received my " safe-conduct," duly signed and magnificently sealed.

The object of my journey was thus accomplished; I returned home in good spirits; and, thanks to Harmony, that amiable daughter of Heaven, my ascension was postponed for a good number of years.

THE CURBS OMELETTE.

Every one knows that for twenty years Madame

E occupied unchallenged the throne of beauty at Paris. It is also known that she was as charitable as she was beautiful, and that she took a great interest in every work of benevolence.

Wishing to consult the Cure of, respecting some charity, she went to his house at five in the afternoon, and was astounded to find him already at table.

Madame Eecamier, Savarins cousin.

Madame E was about to retire, but the cure requested her to stay, as it would by no means interfere with his repast. The table was laid with a neat white cloth; some good old wine sparkled in a decanter of crystal; the white porcelain was of the best quality; the plates had heaters of boiling water under them, and a neatly dressed servant-maid was in attendance.

The repast was limitrophe between frugality and luxury. A crawfish soup had just been removed, and there was on the table a salmon-trout, an omelette, and a salad.

"My dinner will tell you," said the worthy cure with a smile, " that it is fast-day, according to the regulations of our Church." Our fair friend bowed; though a private note tells me the colour somewhat came to her cheek, which, however, did not prevent the cure from eating.

The execution commenced by the trout, the sauce of which betrayed a skilful hand, and the countenance of the cure denoted satisfaction.

After this first dish he attacked the omelette, which was round, pretty thick, and cooked to a point.

At the first incision of the spoon, a thick rich juice issued forth, pleasant to the eye as well as to the smell; the dish seemed full of it, and Madame E owns it made her mouth water.

This sympathetic movement did not escape the cure, accustomed to watch the passions of man, and as if answering a question which Madame

B never put, "It is an omelette au thon,"

(tunny omelette) he said, " and few people taste it without lavishing praises upon it." " I am not surprised at it," rejoined the fair denizen of the Chausee-dantin, "I have never seen so enticing an omelette on our worldly tables."

The salad followed. " I take this opportunity," says Savarin, " of recommending salad to every one who places confidence in me; salad refreshens without weakening, and comforts without irritating; I usually say it regenerates." The dinner did not prevent conversation, and the matter in hand was duly discussed. Other topics were mooted. Dessert, consisting of three apples, a cheese, and a pot of preserves, followed, after which the maid brought up a cup of hot coffee. After having sipped his coffee, the cure said grace. " I never," he said, " take spirits; I always offer liqueurs to my guests, but reserve the use of them for my old age, should it please Providence to let me live so long." The clock struck six, and

Madame R, who had a dinner-party that day, had to hasten to her carriage to be in time to receive her guests, of which I was one. She, " as usual," arrived late, but did arrive at last, quite full of all she had seen and smelt. The cures dinner, but especially the omelette, monopolised the whole conversation during dinner. Madame

E discussed its size, appearance, and odour; and as all the data were from personal observation, it was agreed it must have been a first-rate omelette. Each guest ate it in imagination.

The matter finally dropped, and the conversation turned to other subjects. I, however, the propagator of useful truths, feel it a duty to withdraw from obscurity a preparation which I believe to be as wholesome as it is agreeable. I gave instructions to my chef to get the recipe with the most minute particulars; and I give it the more readily to amateurs, as I do not believe it is to be found in any cookery-book.

HOW TO MAKE AN " OMELETTE AH THON."

Take, for six persons, the roes of two carp; bleach them by putting them for five minutes in boiling water slightly salt.

Take a piece of fresh tunny, about the size of a hens egg, to which add-a small eschalot already chopped.

Hash up together the roe and the tunny so as to mix them well, and throw the whole into a saucepan, with a sufficient piece of very good butter; whip it up till the butter is melted. This constitutes the speciality of the omelette.

Take a second piece of butter, a discretion, mix it with parsley and chives, place it in a long-shaped dish destined to receive the omelette, squeeze the juice of a lemon over it, and place it on hot embers.

Beat up twelve eggs (the fresher the better), throw in the saute of roe and tunny, stirring it so as to mix all well together.

Then make your omelette in the usual manner, endeavouring to turn it out long, thick, and soft. Spread it carefully on the dish prepared for it, and serve up at once.

This dish ought to be reserved for recherche dejeuners, or for assemblies where amateurs meet who know how to eat well; washed down with a good old wine, it will work wonders.

Note. The roe and the tunny must be beaten up (saute) without allowing them to boil, to pre-

vent their hardening, which would prevent them mixing well with the eggs.

Your dish ought to be hollow towards the centre, to allow the gravy to concentrate, that it may be helped with a spoon.

The dish ought to be slightly heated, otherwise the cold china would extract all the heat from the omelette.

EGGS FRIED IN GRAVY.

I was travelling one day with two ladies to Melun. We left rather late in the forenoon, and reached Montgeron with a famous appetite. "We put up at a very decent-looking inn, but, to our disappointment, were informed three diligences and two post-chaises had passed, and the travellers had eaten up everything, like locusts from Egypt

We had, however, looked into the kitchen, and saw a very nice-looking gigot of mutton turning on the spit, towards which the ladies cast hungry-eyes. It belonged to three travellers in the coffee-room.

With a half-angry, half-supplicating voice, I asked whether we could not have some eggs fried in the gravy; with a cup of coffee it would suffice. Oh! certainly." The cook broke the eggs into the dripping-pan. As soon as he turned his back, I maliciously drew my travelling-knife, and made two or three incisions in the roast to allow the juice to flow more freely. I then watched my eggs, and, when they were done, took them to my party. They were found excellent, and we certainly had the best part of the mutton.

A DINNEK AT NEW-YORK.

During my sojourn at New-York (says Savarin), I sometimes used to spend my evenings at a coffeehouse and tavern, kept by one Little, who gave turtle-soup in the morning, and in the evening the refreshments customary in the United States.

I was generally accompanied by Viscount de la Massue and Jean Eodolphe Fehr, formerly a broker at Marseilles, both emigres like myself. We used to have a Welsh-rarebit, and a glass of ale or cider, and talk of the misfortunes of our country, of our pleasures, and our hopes.

Here I made the acquaintance of a Mr. Wilkinson, a Jamaica planter, and of a person who always accompanied him, but whose name I never learnt. He was one of the most extraordinary-looking men I ever met in my life. He had a massive square head, bright eyes, and appeared to examine everything with great attention; but he never spoke, and his features were as rigid as those of a blind man. Only, when anything funny or amusing was said, he would open his mouth as wide as a trap-door, his face would lengthen, and he would give a loud hoarse laugh; as soon as he shut his trap-door, his features became rigid again. It was like a flash of lightning through a dark cloud. As regards Mr. Wilkinson, who appeared about fifty years of age, he had all the manners and appearance of a perfect gentleman.

Savarin naively enough calls this a lupin gallois.

These two Englishmen seemed to take pleasure in our society, and had more than once shared the frugal repast I sometimes offered to my friends. One evening Mr. Wilkinson took me aside, and said he hoped I and my two friends would do him the pleasure of dining with him.

I accepted for myself and friends, and the dinner was to be on the day after the morrow.

The evening passed as usual, but as I was leaving, the waiter took me aside and told me that the "Jamaica gentlemen" had ordered a good dinner, but had given particular orders about the wines, because they looked upon their invitation as a challenge who could drink most, and that the man with the large mouth had said that he hoped he alone could drink the Frenchmen under the table.

This information would have induced me at once to send an excuse, if I could honourably have done so, for I hate such orgies, but it was out of the question. The Englishmen would have proclaimed everywhere that we shirked, and that their presence alone sufficed to appal us; and therefore, though prewarned, we followed the maxim of Marshal Saxe: the wine was drawn, and we resolved to drink it.

I was not without some anxiety; but not on my own account. I knew that being younger, bigger, and more vigorous than our Amphitryons, my constitution, uninjured by bacchanalian excesses, was a match for the two Englishmen; but, though I might have come off victorious, that victory would have been greatly lessened by the defeat of my two companions. Consequently, I held a sort of council of war with Fehre and Massue. I recommended them to drink as little as possible, above all things, to eat slowly, and to preserve a little p appetite throughout, because food mixed with drink moderates the effect, and prevents its rushing to the head so strongly. Finally, we ate between us a plate of bitter almonds, which I believe have the peculiarity of obviating to a certain extent the effects of intoxicating liquors.

Thus armed, physically and morally, we proceeded to Littles, where we found the Jamaicans ready to receive us. Dinner was served up at once. It consisted of a huge roast of beef, boiled vegetables, a roast turkey, salad, and a fruit tart. The beverage was excellent claret. Mr. Wilkinson did the honours well, encouraging us-to eat, and setting us the example; his friend seemed lost in the bottom of his plate, did not say a word, but there was a sly smile on the corner of his lips.

I felt proud of ray two companions. La Massue, who was gifted with a great appetite, ate like a petite mattresse, and Fehre emptied his glass once or twice into a beer-jug near him. For my part, I drank glass for glass with the Englishmen, and as the dinner progressed I felt my confidence increase.

After the claret we had Port, then Madeira, which was passed round briskly.

The dessert consisted of fresh butter, cheese, cocoa, and hickory nuts. Toasts were proposed. We drank the health of kings, the liberty of nations, the beauty of women. Mr. Wilkinson proposed the health of his daughter, which we drank in bumpers.

After the wine, spirits were brought in; that is to say, rum, brandy, and gin. We now sang songs: I saw it was getting hot. I feared the spirits; I avoided taking any by asking for punch. Little himself brought in a mighty bowl, evidently brewed beforehand, which would have sufficed for forty persons. I have never seen a bowl of such dimensions in France.

This gave me new courage; I ate five or six slices of well-buttered toast, and felt my head quite clear. I now cast a scrutinising glance around me, for I began to feel anxious how it would terminate. My two friends appeared steady enough, were sipping their punch and eating hickory nuts. Mr. Wilkinsons face was a purple-red, and his eyes unsteady,–he seemed to have had enough; his friend was silent, as usual, but his head fumed like a boiler. I saw the crisis was coming.

Mr. Wilkinson suddenly roused himself, and in a sonorous tone struck up "Eule, Britannia;" but before he had got through the first verse, he lost his balance, reeled off his chair, and slipped under the table. His friend gave one of his deep laughs, and stooped to help him, fell over, and could not get up again.

My mind was greatly relieved at this brusque denouement. I pulled the bell; Little came up himself, and I gave the usual phrase, "See that these gentlemen are properly taken care of." We had a glass of punch with Little to their health. The waiters came in, and seizing upon the vanquished, carried them off, feet foremost; Wilkinson still endeavouring to sing " Eule, Britannia;" his friend, as usual, silent.

The New York papers got wind of the affair, and it went the round of all the papers of the Union. Hearing that Mr. Wilkinson was laid up from the effects of the dinner, I went to see him, which seemed to give him great pleasure. He was suffering from a severe attack of gout, and, shaking me by the hand when I left, said:–

"My dear Sir, you are very good company, but too hard a drinker for us/

CLASSICAL GOURMANDISE.

Under the title of " History of M. de Borose," Savarin gives some valuable hints on the " Art of Eating." As a dinner-giver, M. de Borose acquired a reputation at Paris; of independent fortune and good position in society, he made it an object to make his dinners as perfect as possible. This became so well known, that when a butcher or victualler had a choice piece of meat or game, he would prefer letting M. de Borose have it at a fair price to selling it at a high price anywhere else, simply because he knew its merits would be discussed by competent judges, and his shop be sought after.

With Epicurus, M. de Borose said:–

"Is man to disdain the gifts of nature? Is he placed on earth to cull only bitter fruits? For whom are the flowers the gods ordain to grow beneath the feet of mortals? It is pleasing to Providence that we should give way to the inclinations it suggests to us; our duties emanate from its laws; our desires from its inspirations."

A little time, reflection, and experience soon taught M. de Borose that, the number of dishes being almost limited by custom, a good dinner ought not to cost much more than a bad one; that it does not cost 201. a year more whether you give good or bad wine; and that everything depends on the will of the master, the order he keeps in his household, and the authority he exercises over his servants.

Starting from these fundamental points, Boroses dinners acquired a classical reputation; men took pains to get invited, and some talked about them who had never been there. He never asked a soi-dieant gastronome who was a glutton and who ate wholesale. He invited men of intellect and taste, who knew what was good, and never forgot the maxim which reason says to appetite: " non precedes amplius"

His dinner-parties seldom exceeded nine, and the dishes were not very numerous; but his care and exquisite taste made them perfect. At all seasons of the year his table presented the best that was to be had, and you were waited upon with such attention that it left nothing to be desired.

The conversation during dinner was always general, amusing, often instructive; this latter quality was due to a very peculiar precaution of Borose. Once a week a learned friend of his, to whom he gave a salary, used to give him subjects fit for discussion at table. De Borose used cleverly to turn the conversation to the subject. Twice a week he invited ladies, and always took care that each lady had a cavalier into whose charge he placed her. This precaution greatly enhanced the pleasure of the evening, because even the severest prude feels humiliated if no notice is taken of her. Music and icarte whiled away the evening.

On the first Monday of every month, De Borose made a point of asking his parish clergyman. On that day the conversation assumed a tone a little more serious, but did not exclude innocent gaiety. The worthy pastor has been heard to say, that he wished there were four first Mondays in every month.

Borose was very particular as to whom he dealt with. He insisted upon a first-rate article, and a moderate price. He would lend money to his providers, if times were bad, as long as he found they were honest, and served him well. He made the fortune of his wine-merchant, by proclaiming him a man who did not adulterate his wines, a quality already rare at Athens in the days of Pericles, and scarcely to be found at the present day.

He did not allow anything at his table to be wasted or taken as perquisites by bis servants, whom he paid liberally. He gave away bis broken meat in charity.

The above few lines contain within them nearly the whole art of giving dinners.

CHAP. XIII.

Thk following chapter scarcely comes under the head of " The Art of Eating;" yet it is intimately connected with it. Savarin was no mean proficient in the medical science, and had made himself master of the structure of the human frame. He had studied it theoretically and practically. The conclusions he came to on various points more nearly affecting the health of man, are most valuable, and will be read with interest even by the " Faculty." Sufficient will-have already transpired in the preceding chapters to prove to the reader that Savarin was a man of superior mind, of deep thought, and, moreover, highly practical in his deductions. Many a valuable hint may be taken, by both sexes, from the few following pages.

ON DIGESTION.

"We do not live (says an old adage) upon what ive eat, but upon what we digest." To live, therefore, we must digest, and this rule is applicable to the rich as to the poor, to the peasant as to the king.

But how few men are acquainted with the functions of digestion. Thoroughly to understand them, they ought to be studied in their antecedents and in their consequences.

We shall not follow M. Savarin in his scientific description of those organs of the human frame more intimately connected with the digestive functions and of those functions themselves, but come to his conclusions.

Digestion is of all the functions of our body that one which has the most influence on the morale of the individual.

The principles of the most simple psychology teach us that the mind is acted upon by the organs which are subject to it, and which place it in contact with external objects; hence it comes, that when those organs are out of order, badly restored, or irritated, that state of degradation exercises a necessary influence on the sensations which are the intermediary and occasional means of intellectual operations.

Thus, without our being aware of it, and, what is more, without our being able to prevent it. accordingly as we digest are we sad, gay, taciturn, lively, morose, or melancholy.

Young persons will sometimes shiver after dinner, and elderly persons feel inclined to go to sleep.

In the first instance, it is nature which withdraws the caloric from the surface to employ it in its laboratory; in the second, it is the same power which, already enfeebled by age, cannot suffice at the same time for the work of digestion and the keeping up of the sensations.

In the first moments of digestion, it is bad, even dangerous, to do mental work or commit any excess. This is applicable to youth, as well as to middle and old age. Some people are invariably in a bad temper whilst digestion is going on; if men in power, this is not the time to propose a plan, or ask a favour from them.

On Repose.

Man is not meant to enjoy indefinite activity; nature has only destined him to an interrupted existence; his perceptions finish after a given time. The period of activity may be lengthened by varying the form and nature of the sensations he experiences; but that continuity of existence leads him to desire repose. Eepose leads to sleep, and sleep brings dreams.

Shelleys beautiful lines will rise before the reader:–

"How wonderful is Death,

Death and his brother Sleep !

One, pale as yonder waning moon,

With lips of lurid blue;

The other, rosy as the morn

When throned on Oceans wave, It blushes oer the world:

Yet both so passing wonderful! "

But to return to Savarin.

We have now reached the last limits of humanity. For the man who sleeps is no longer a social being; the law still protects him, but commands him no longer.

The general laws imposed upon the globe which we inhabit have necessarily influenced the mode of life of the human species. The change of day and night which is felt upon the whole earth with certain varieties, but still sufficiently to compensate each other, has naturally enough indicated the time for activity and for rest; and, probably, the use of our life would not have been the same if we had been given day without end.

However this may be, when a man has for a certain length of time enjoyed the fulness of life, he begins to feel weary; his impressions become less vivid; in vain he strives to keep his senses alive; the organs refuse compliance; the soul is saturated with sensation; the hour of rest is at hand.

The reader will observe that we are here considering social man surrounded by all the resources of comfort and high civilisation, for the want of sleep comes much quicker and much more regularly to the man who undergoes assiduous labour, or to men who have made a long journey, been on the battle-field, at the chase, or who have gone through any other great exertion.

And Nature, that excellent mother, has endowed sleep, like her other gifts, with great pleasure.

The man who reposes experiences an inexpressible feeling of happiness; his arms fall from their own weight, his muscles relax, his brain feels light, his senses are calm, his sensations deadened; he desires nothing, he does not think; a veil of gauze is drawn over his sight. A few moments more,–he sleeps.

There are some men so organised that it may almost be said they do not sleep at all, yet the general truth is that the want of sleep is as imperious as hunger or thirst. The outposts of an army often fall asleep, even though they throw snuff into their eyes. Pichegru, when tracked by the police of Bonaparte, gave 30,000 francs for a nights sleep, and that very night he was betrayed and given up.

Like all other pleasures, sleep may be carried to an extreme. Men have been known to have slept away three quarters of their life; the effects in such case are baneful:–idleness, indolence, weakness, stupidity, and death.

The school of Salerno allowed seven hours sleep to all ages and sexes. That doctrine is too severe; children and women require more; but more than ten hours in bed is always an excess.

And what does the mind do during this lapse? It lives in itself; it is like a pilot in a calm, as a mirror in the night, a lute, the strings of which vibrate not to a touch; it awaits fresh excitement.

There are, however, some psychologists, amongst others Count de Eedern, who maintain that the mind never ceases to act, and the latter supports his opinion on the ground that every man aroused from his first sleep experiences the sensation of one disturbed in some serious occupation.

There is some truth in the observation, which is worth investigation.

THE INFLUENCE OF DIET ON UEST, SLEEP, AND DREAMS.

Whether a man rests, sleeps, or dreams, he does not cease to be under the power of the laws of nutrition, and does not leave the limits of the empire of Gastronomy.

Theory and experience agree to prove that the quality and the quantity of food exercise a powerful influence upon labouv, repose, sleep, and dreams.

An ill-fed man cannot support the fatigue of prolonged labour; he perspires; his strength leaves him; and, for him, repose is simply the impossibility of action.

If it is a mental labour, the ideas are weak and vacillating; reflection refuses its aid, and judgment fails; the brain wearies itself in vain efforts, and the writer dozes off.

On the other hand, the man who lives well, and is careful of himself, will do an amount of labour scarcely credible.

Diet has no less influence on sleep and dreams. A hungry man cannot sleep; the pains in his stomach keep him in a painful state of sleeplessness. On the other hand, the man who has eaten too much, falls at once into a heavy sleep; if he dreams, he has no recollection of what he dreamt about. He awakes suddenly, and it is some time before he is again restored to social life; and when the heaviness of sleep has quite left him, he still suffers, for a long time, from want of digestion.

As a general maxim, it may be said that coffee drives away sleep. Custom obviates the effect; but it infallibly has this effect upon all Europeans who are not accustomed to it. Some articles of food, on the contrary, promote sleep, namely, all those where milk predominates, chicken, orange-flower, and especially a rennet apple, if eaten just before bed-time.

Experience, supported by a thousand facts, shows that diet determines dreams. Generally speaking, all articles of food of an exciting nature cause dreams, more especially pigeons, ducks, game, and especially hare. The same may be said of asparagus, celery, truffles, perfumed sweets, and especially vanille.

It would be a great error to suppose that all these things ought to be banished from the table; for the dreams they occasion are generally speaking agreeable, and prolong our existence, even during our sleep. There are persons for whom sleep is a sort of separate existence, a sort of prolonged romance; that is to say, their dreams are continued from night to night, and they recognise old faces, which, however, they never meet in the real world.

The man who reflects upon his physical existence, and regulates it according to the principles which we develope, that man will carefully prepare his repose, his sleep, and his dreams. He will divide his labour so as not to overwork himself; he will make it lighter by variety, and refreshen himself by short intervals of rest which relieve him without interrupting his train of thoughts. If sometimes he should find a longer rest than usual necessary, let him take it in a sitting posture; let him rest without sleeping, unless quite overcome, and let him especially avoid acquiring the habit of it.

When he retires to bed at the usual hour, let his bedroom be airy, let him not draw the bed-curtains close, which would make him breathe continually the same air; and let him not close his shutters completely, so that whenever his eye opens it may be comforted by a ray of light.

Let his pillows be slightly raised; his pillow Q ought to be of horse-hair, his nightcap of linen; his chest not oppressed with bed-clothes, but let his feet be warmly covered.

He has eaten well, but not too much; he has drunk the best wines, abstemiously, even of the very best. At dessert he has talked of gallantry more than of politics; he has taken a cup of coffee, and perhaps a glass of liqueur after it. He has been an amiable companion, and has afterwards spent a pleasant evening where music has prevailed. He retires to rest satisfied with himself and others, his eyes close, and he falls into deep calm sleep. Nature is soon relieved. Pleasant dreams hover round him and impart a mysterious existence; he sees the persons he loves, finds his favourite occupations, and rambles amongst his favourite haunts.

Finally, sleep leaves his eyelids, and he returns to society without regretting the time lost, because, even in his sleep, he has enjoyed activity without fatigue, pleasure without alloy.

ORESITY OR EMBONPOINT.

The primary cause of embonpoint is the natural disposition of the individual. Most men are born with certain predispositions which are stamped upon their features. Out of one hundred persons who die of consumption, ninety have brown hair, a long face, and a sharp nose. Out of one hundred fat ones, ninety have short faces, round eyes, and a short nose.

Consequently there are persons whose destiny it is to be fat. This physical truth has often given me annoyance. I have at times met in society some dear little creature with rounded arms, dimpled cheeks and hands, and pert little nose, fresh and blooming, the admiration of every one, when, taught by experience, I cast a rapid mental glance through the next ten years of her life, and I behold those charms in another light, and I sigh internally. This anticipated compassion is a painful feeling, and gives one more proof that man would be very unhappy if he could foresee the future.

The second and chief cause of obesity is to be found in the mealy or floury substance of which man makes his food. All animals that live on farinaceous food grow fat; man follows the common law. Mixed with sugar the fattening qualities increase. Beer is very fattening. Too much sleep and little exercise will promote corpulency. Another cause of obesity is in eating and drinking too much.

M. Louis Greffulhe called upon me one day and said that having heard I was writing a treatise on obesity, and he was very much inclined to be corpulent, he should feel obliged to me for advice.

"My dear Sir," I said, " not having taken out a regular diploma, I might refuse to advise you, but if you will give me your word of honour to follow for one month the instructions I give you, I will tell you what to do."

He promised to do so. I gave him my instructions, requesting him to have himself weighed at once, and again at the expiration of the month.

When the month was out, M. Greffulhe came to see me, and spoke to the following intent:–

"Sir, I have followed your instructions to the letter, as if my life depended upon it, and during the month I have lost more than three pounds of flesh. But, to obtain that result, I have been obliged forcibly to gainsay all my tastes, all my customs,–in a word, I have suffered so much, that whilst I give you my best thanks for your good advice, I now renounce all benefit I might derive from following it, and shall allow Providence to deal with me as it thinks fit."

It grieved me to hear this, for I feared the result; M. Greffulhe grew more and more corpulent, and, before he reached his fortieth year, died of suffocation.

To cure embonpoint (obesity, corpulency) you must commence by these three precepts of absolute theory,–discretion in eating; moderation in sleep; exercise on horseback or on foot.

These are the first resources that science offers us; but I count little upon them, because I have a knowledge of men and things, and know that if a prescription is not carried out to the letter it cannot produce the desired effect.,

Now, 1st, it requires a firm will to leave the dinner-table with an appetite; as long as the craving is felt, one morsel invokes another with irresistible attraction, and, generally speaking, we eat as long as we are hungry, despite the doctors, and even the example of doctors.

2nd. To tell a person of embonpoint to get up early in the morning, is to break his (or her) heart; they will tell you it will ruin their health; that if they get up early, they are not fit for anything during the rest of the day; the ladies will

complain that their eyes look heavy; they will all consent to sit up late, but they must have a long snooze in the morning; and here is one resource lost 3rd. Kiding is a dear remedy, which does not suit every fortune or every position.

Propose to a pretty fat girl to ride, she will consent with delight, but on three conditions–she must have a pretty and quiet horse, a well-made habit of the last fashion, and a handsome fellow to ride with. Now, these three things are not always to be had, so riding is given up.

Walking has many other objections. It is so fatiguing, the mud and the dust are dreadful, and the stones cut the pretty little boots, and then, if a pimple, the size of a pins head, should break out, it is immediately put down to that horrid doctor and his system, which is, of course, abandoned.

Of all medical powers, diet is the most efficient, because it acts incessantly, day and night, sleeping or waking; it ends by subjugating the individual.

Now, the diet against corpulency is indicated by the most common and active cause of obesity; and as it has been proved that farinaceous food produces fat, in man as well as in animals, it may be concluded that abstinence from farinaceous substances tends to diminish embonpoint.

I hear my fair friends exclaim that I am a monster, who wishes to deprive them of everything they like. Let them not be alarmed.

If they must eat bread, let it be brown bread; it is very good, but not so nutritious as white bread.

If you are fond of soup, have it a la julienne or with vegetables, but no paste, no macaroni.

At the first course eat anything you like, except the rice with fowls, or the crust of pates.

The second course requires more philosophy. Avoid everything farinaceous. You can eat roast, salad, and vegetables. And if you must needs have some sweets, take chocolate, creams, and gelees, and punch in preference to orange or others.

Now comes dessert. New danger. But if you have been prudent so far, you will continue to be so. Avoid biscuits and macaroons; eat as much fruit as you like.

After dinner take a cup of coffee and a glass of liqueur. Tea and punch will not hurt you.

At breakfast brown bread and chocolate in preference to coffee. No eggs. Anything else you like. You cannot breakfast too early. If you breakfast late, the dinner hour comes before you have properly digested; you do not eat the less, and this eating without an appetite is a prime cause of obesity; because it often occurs.

The above regulations are to prevent embonpoint, the following are for those who are already victims.

Drink, every summer, thirty bottles of Seltzer water, a large tumblerful every morning, two hours before breakfast, and the same before. you go to bed. Drink white wines and rather acid. Avoid beer like the plague. Eat radishes, artichokes, celery; eat veal and chicken in preference to beef and mutton; only eat the crust of your bread; you will be all the lighter and younger for it.

I must now warn you against a danger which extra zeal might lead you into. That danger is the habitual use of acids, which ignorant people sometimes recommend, and which experience has shown to have very baneful effects.

This dreadful doctrine prevails amongst ladies, and the idea that acids,-especially vinegar, will prevent embonpoint, carries many a fair girl to an early grave.

There is no doubt a continual use of acids will make a person thin; but it destroys their freshness, their health, their life; even lemonade, which is the mildest of them, will gradually do harm.

This truth cannot be made too public; many readers could give me examples to support it. I will only give one case which came under my own personal observation.

In 1776 I lived at Dijon; I was studying law chemistry, and medicine.

I had a Platonic friendship for one of the most charming persons I have ever met. Louise –was a lovely girl, and had that classical embonpoint which charms the eye and is the glory of sculptors.

Though only a friend, I was not blind to her attractions, and this is perhaps why I observed her so closely. " Chere amie," I said to her one evening, "you are not well; you seem to be thinner." " Oh! no," she said, with a smile which partook of melancholy, "I am very well; and if I am a little thinner I can very well afford it." " Afford it! " I said, with warmth; " you can afford neither to gain nor lose; remain beautiful as you are," and other phrases pardonable to a young man of twenty.

that conversation, I watched her more closely with an interest not untinged with anxiety; gradually I saw her cheeks fall in, her figure decline. One evening at a ball, after dancing a quadrille, I cross-questioned her, and she reluctantly avowed that, her school friends having laughed at her, and told her that in two years she would be as fat as St. Christopher, she had for more than a month drunk a glass of vinegar every morning; she added that she had not told anybody of it.

I shuddered when I heard her confession; I was aware of the danger she incurred, and next day I informed her mother, who was terribly alarmed, for she doted upon her child. No time was lost. The very best advice was taken. All in vain! The springs of life had been attacked at the source; and when the danger was suspected, all hope was already gone.

Thus, for having followed an ignorant advice, poor Louise was carried to her grave in her eighteenth year, her last days embittered by the thought that she herself, involuntarily, had cut short her existence.

She was the first person I ever saw die; she died in my arms, as, at her wish, I was raising her up that she might behold the light. Some days after her death, I accompanied her bereaved mother to take a last glance at her countenance. With surprise we observed that a radiant almost an ecstatic expression was on her features, which was not there when she died. I was astonished. The mother drew from it a favourable augury; but this is not a rare occurrence; Lavater mentions it in his " Treatise on Physiognomy."

Savarin recommends a belt to be worn round the waist, to be gradually tightened as corpulency decreases. He himself wore one with effect for six years. He recommends bark (quinquina) as conducive to reduce embonpoint, a teaspoonful in a glass of white wine about two hours before breakfast.

ON LEANNESS.

There are two sorts of leanness. The first is that which, being the result of the primitive disposition of the body, is accompanied by the full health and exercise of all the organic functions, the second is that which, having for cause the weakness of certain organs or the defective action of others, gives a sickly and miserable appearance to the individual. I knew a young lady of the middle size, who only weighed sixty-five pounds.

Leanness is no disadvantage to a man. He is every bit as strong and more active. The father of the young person I just mentioned, although very thin, was so strong that he could take a chair in his teeth and throw it over his head.

But it is a great disaster for ladies, for beauty is their life, and beauty consists chiefly in the rounded limb and graceful curve. The most re-cherche toilet, the best dressmaker in the world, cannot supply certain absences, or hide certain angles. But a woman who is born thin may be fattened like a chicken. It may take more time. The ladies must pardon me the simile, but I could not find a better.

Every thin woman would like to be fat: we have heard the wish expressed a thousand times; it is as a homage to that all-powerful sex that we shall endeavour to replace by real forms those inventions which in the shop-windows shock the sight of the passer by.

The whole secret how to get fat consists in a suitable diet. You must know " how to eat," and how to select your food.

Let us, then, put down the daily food of some sylph or sylphide that wishes to increase in corpulence.

General Rule. –Eat a quantity of fresh bread–the same days baking–and do not. throw away the crumb.

Before eight A. M., when in bed, take a basin of soup (potage au pain or aux pates), not too much, or, if you prefer it, a cup of good chocolate.

Breakfast at eleven. Fresh eggs, boiled or poached, pet its pates, cutlets, or anything else; but eggs are essential. A cup of coffee will not hurt.

After breakfast take a little exercise. Go shopping, or call on a friend, sit and chat, and walk home again.

At dinner, eat as much soup, meat, and fish as you like, but do not omit to eat the rice with the fowl, macaroni, sweet pastry, creams, andc.

At dessert, savoy biscuits, babas, and other farinaceous preparations which contain eggs and sugar.

This diet may seem limited, but it is capable of great variation, and comprises the whole animal kingdom.

Drink beer by preference; otherwise Bordeaux, or wine from the South of France.

Avoid acids; except salad, which gladdens the heart. Eat sugar with your fruit, if it admits of it. Do not take baths too cold; breathe the fresh air of the country as often as you can; eat plenty of grapes when in season; do not fatigue yourself by dancing at a ball.

Go to bed at eleven oclock; on extra nights be in bed by one.

If this system is boldly and exactly adhered to, the failings of nature will soon be supplied; health and beauty will be the result.

We fatten sheep, calves, oxen, poultry, carp, crawfish, oysters, whence I deduct the general maxim:

"Everything that eats can be fattened, provided the food is well and suitably chosen."
Fasting.

Fasting is a voluntary abstention from food, with a moral or religious object.

Although contrary to our inclinations, or rather to our habitual wants, it is nevertheless of great antiquity.

It originated in cases of private affliction. If a father, a mother, a beloved child died in a family, the whole house was in mourning; they wept, they washed and embalmed the body, and it was buried with the honours due to the rank of the deceased. On these occasions men cared little for eating; they fasted without being aware of it.

In like manner, in cases of great public calamities, in great droughts or incessant rains, cruel wars or dire pestilences, in a word, in the case of scourges against which toil and industry were of no avail, men gave themselves up to lamentations, and imputed the disasters to the anger of the gods; they humiliated themselves before them, and mortified the flesh by fasting. The scourges ceased, and this was attributed to the offerings and fasting, and on future occasions they were again had recourse to.

Thus men afflicted by public or private calamities, gave themselves up to sorrow, and neglected to take food; ultimately, they looked upon this voluntary, abstinence as an act of religion.

They thought that by macerating their body, when mind was in sorrow, they would move the pity of the gods, and this idea taken up by all nations, led to mourning, offerings, prayers, sacrifices, mortifications, and abstinence.

Finally, our Saviour sanctified fasting, and all Christian sects have adopted it with more or less mortifications.

Fasting has considerably fallen off, and there are. some persons of such delicate constitution that it is death to them. Here gastronomy steps in to their relief.

A man who has undergone great muscular exertion, ought to take a good basin of soup, some generous wine, meat, and sleep.

A literary man, who excited by his subject has fatigued himself, should seek the open air, take a warm bath, dine on fowl and vegetables, and take repose.

ON DEATH.

"Omnia mors poscit; lex est, non pcena, perire."

The Creator has imposed upon man six grand and principal necessities, which are, birth, action, eating, sleep, reproduction, and death.

Death is the absolute interruption of sensual relations and the complete extinction of the vital power, which leaves the body to the laws of decomposition.

These various necessities are all accompanied and softened by pleasurable sensations, and eveii death is not without charms when it is natural, that is to say, when the body has gone through the different phases of growth, virility, old age, and decrepitude, to which it is destined. When Fontenelle was dying, he was asked how he felt: " Simply a difficulty to live," he replied.

I was (says Savarin) at the death-bed of an old aunt, watching over her with tenderness. "Are you there, my nephew?" she said, with a voice scarcely audible. "Yes, my aunt, and I think a glass of generous wine would do you good." " Give it to me, mon ami. I can swallow that." I gave her half a glass of my best wine. She seemed to revive at once, and looking at me with eyes which were once very fine, she said:

"Thanks for this last service; if ever you attain my age, you will feel that death is quite as necessary as sleep." These were the last words she ever spoke. Half an hour afterwards she slept the long sleep of death.

Schiller, in his master-poem " Die Kiinstler," has a beautiful allegory on Life and Death. He compares the life of man to an arch, that is to say, to an imperfect portion of a circle, which is continued throughout the night of the tomb to complete the circle. Now the young moon is such an arch, and the remainder of the circle is not visible. He places two youths side by side, the one with a lighted torch, the other with his torch extinguished; the former he compares to that portion of the moon which is light, and the latter with that part which is in darkness.

The Artists. Very ably translated by our present Secretary for the Colonies, Bulwer Lytton. R

"Da zeigte sich mit umgesturztem Lichte,
An Kastor angelehnt, ein bliihend Pollnx-Bild."

Ossian, speaking of a man at deaths door,

"Death stood hehind him like the dark side of the moon behind its silver horn."

Dr. Eicherand has described with so much truth and philosophy the last degradations of the human body, and the last moments of the individual, that my readers will thank me for the following extract:–

" Der Schattenin des Mondes Angesichte." " The shadow in the Moons pale glimmer seen."

"The intellectual faculties leave as follows: Eeason, that quality of which man pretends to be the exclusive possessor, abandons him the first. He first loses the power of expressing a judgment and then of connecting his ideas. It is then said he has lost his head,–that he is talking wildly,–that he is delirious. In this state, his favourite ideas prevail, his dominating passion betrays itself. The miser mumbles about his hoarded gold, and betrays where his hidden treasures lie concealed; another dies in religious torments. Another, in touching words, dwells upon the delights of his distant country. Great weakness is the next step. Memory then goes. The dying man, who even in his delirium could recognise who approached him, now does not know his dearest relations. Soon all feeling is lost; but the senses expire in a successive and fixed order: taste and smell no longer give any sign of existence; a veil comes over the eye, and it has a dull appearance; the ear is still sensible to noise and sound. This is why, probably, the ancients used to scream into the ears of the dead. The dying man who has lost taste, smell and hearing, still feels; he is restless on his couch, puts his arms out; he has no pain, he fears not death, his ideas are gone, and he ceases to live as he commenced to live, without knowing how."

"Pallida Mors sequo pulsat pede pauperum tabernas,
Reguraque turres."

END-

PEINTED BY SPOTTI8WOODH AND CO.
NEW-STBEET SQUABE.

OF
20
Cecils Stud Farm 8

21
22
32
21
Lows Elements of Agriculture. 14
Morton on Landed Estates.17
22
23
Brandes Dictionary of Science, Ac. 0
Fairbairns Information for Engineers. 9
Jumesons Sacred and Legendary Art 12, 13
Piesses Art of Perfumery. 18
16
Scoffern on Projectiles, Ac.20
Scmenor on the Iron Trade.20
16
15
r res Dictionary of Arts, andc.23
19
Gleigs Essays. 10
20
Lardners Cabinet Cyclopedia. 13
Maunders Biographical Treasury. 15
Mountains (Col.) Memoirs. 17
Parrys (Admiral) Memoirs. 18
24
24
24
24

NEW WORKS IN GENERAL LITERATURE
PUBLISHED BY
LON0MAN, BROWN, 0REEN, LON0MANS, AND ROBERTS
39 Paternoster Kow, London.

CLASSIFIED INDEX
Agriculture and Rural Affairs.
Russells Memoirs of Moore.
"(Dr.) Life of Mezzofanti.
16
Bayldon on Valuing Rents, andc. 5
Schimmelpennincks (Mrs.) Life.
Southeys Life of Wesley
20
Hoskvnss Talpa 11
"Life and Correspondence
Stephens Ecclesiastical Biography

Lardners Cabinet Cyclopaedia
13
Londons Ladys Country Companion.
Maunders Treasury of Knowledge.
11
Richardsons Art of Horsemanship. 19
"Biographical Treasury
"Geographical Treasury
"Scientific Treasury.
15
Steam Engine, by the Artisan Club. 6
"Treasury of History
"Natural History.
in
u
18
Biography.
Pocket and the Stud.
Pycrofts English Reading.
10
Aragos Lives of Scientific Men. 6
Reeces Medical Guide.
19
Brialmonts Wellington. 6
Richs Companion to Latin Dictionary.
19
Bunsens Hippolytns. 7
Richardsons Art of Horsemanship
Crosses (Andrew) Memorials. 9
Riddles Latin Dictionaries.
19
Rogets English 1 heaaurus.
20
Greens Princesses of England 10
Short Whiat
21
Harfords Life of Michaef Angelo. 10
Thomsons Interest Tables.
Websters Domestic Economy.
West on Childrens Diseases.
"Wtllichs Popular Tables
Wilmots Blackstone.
22

Botany and Gardening. Rosens Eways from Edinb. Review. Rogets English Thesaurus. 20 20

Humlli British Freshwater Alga. 1 1 Schmitzs History of Greece. 20
Hookers British Flora. 1 Seutheyt Doctor 21
"Gaide to Eew Gardens. 1 " " Kew Museum. 1 Stephens Ecclesiastical Biography "
Lectures on French History. 22
22
Lindleys Introduction to Botsny. 1 " Theory of Horticulture. 1 Sydney Smiths Works.
1. tur.-, 21 21
Loudons Hortus Britannicus. 1 "Memoirs 21
tl W 22
"Trees and Shrubs. 14 22
"Gardening.14 Thirlfralls History of Greece. 22
"Plants. 14 Thomass Historical Notes. 27
Pereiras Materia Medica. 18 Townsends State Trials 22
Riverss Rose Amateurs Guide. 19 Turners Anglo-Saxons. 23
Wilsons British Mosses. 24 "Saoz d History of the World. Uwinss Memoirs and
Letters Vehses Austrian Court. Wades Englands Greatness. Youngs Christ of History
"Middle Ages. 23
Chronology. 23 23 23 24
Blairs Chronological Tables. 6 Brewers Historical Atlas. 6 Bunsens Ancient Egypt.
7 I
Calendars of English state Papers. 7
    Haydns Beatsons Index.11
    Jaquemets Chronology. 13
    "Abridged Chronology. 13
    Commerce and Mercantile
Affairs.
    Gilbarts Treatise on Banking. 10
Lorimers "Young Master Mariner. 14
    Macleods Banking 15
    MCullochs Commerce and Navigation 15 Murray on French Finance.18 Scrivenor
on the Iron Trade.20 Thomsons Interest Tables. 22 Tookes History of Prices. 22
    Criticism, History, and Memoirs.
    Blairs Chron. and Historical Tables. 6
    Brewers Historical Atlas. 6
    Bunsens Ancient Egypt. 7
    "Hippolytus. 7
    Calendars of English State Papers. 7
    Capgraves Illustrious Henries,. 8
    Chapmans Gustavus Adolphus. 8
    Chronicles and Memorisls of England. 8
    Connollys Sappers and Miners. 8
    Conybeare and Howsone St. Paul. 8
    Crowes History of France. 9
    Fischers Francis Bacon. 9
    Gleigs Essays 10

Custs Invalidsown Book. 9
Hollands Mental Physiology. 11
"Medical Notes ana" Reflections 11 How to Nurse Sick Children.12
Kestevens Domestic Medicine. 13
Pereiras Materia Medica. 18
Reeces Medical Guide. 19
Richardsons Cold-water Cure. 19
Spencers Principles of Psychology. 21 West on Diseases of Infancy.24
Miscellaneous Literature.
Bacons (Lord) Works. 5
Defence of Eclipse of Faith . 9
Eclipse of Faith S
Greatheds Letters from Delhi. 1O
Greysons Select Correspondence. 1ft
Gurneys Evening Recreations. 10
Hassans Adulterations Detected, Ac. 11 Haydns Book of Dignities.11
Hollands Mental Physiology. 11 Hookers Kew Guides. 11
Howitts Rural Life of England. n
"Visits to Remarksble Places. 12
Jamesons Commonplsce-Book. 13
Jeffreys (Lord) Contributions. 13
Last of the Old Squires. 18 Letters of a Betrothed.13
Macaulsys Critical and Hist. Essays. 14
"Speeches. 14
Mackintoshs Miscellaneous Works. 15
Martineaus Miscellanies. 15
Pycrofts English Reading. 19
Raikes on the Indian Revolt. 19
Reess Siege of Lucknow. 19
Richs Companion to Latin Dictionary 19
Riddles Latin Dictionaries. 19
Rowtons Debster 20
Seawards Narrative of his Shipwreck. 20
Sir Roger De Coverley. 21
Smiths Rev. Sydney) Works. 21
Southeys Doctor, andc 21
Spencers Essays 21
Stephens Essays 22
Stows Training System. 22
Thomsons Laws of Thought. 22 Tighe and Daviss vvindsor.22
Townsends State Trials. 22
Yonges English-Greek Lexicon. 24 " Latin Gradtih.24 . 24
Zumpts Latin Grammar
Natural History in general.
Catlows Popular Concholoey. 8

"Abridgment of ditto-. 11
Hues Christianity in China. 12
Humphreyssp wfl6te Illuminated. 12 Ivors, by the Author of Amy Herbert. 20
Jamesons Saints snd Martyrs. 12
"Monastic Legends. 13
"Legends of the Madonna. 13
"on Fem; ile Employment. 13
Jeremy Taylors Works. 13
Katharine Ashton 21
Konige Pictorial Life of Luther. 10
Laneton Parsonage 20
Letters to my Unknown Friends.13
"on Happiness. 13
Lyra Germanica 7
Maguires Rome 15
Margaret Percival 20
Martineaus Christian Life. 15
"Hymns. 15
"Studies of Christianity. 15
Merivales Christian Records. 16
Milners Church of Christ. 26
Moore on the Use of the Body. 26
"" Soul and Body. 26 t s Man and his Motives. 26
Morning Clouds 17
Neales Closing Scene. 18 Pattisons Earth and Word.18
Powells Christianity without Judaism. 19
Readings for Lent 20
"Confirmation. 20 Riddles Household Prayers. 19 Robinsons Lexicon to the Greek
Testament 20
Saints our Example. 20
Sermon in the Mount. 20
Sinclair Journey of Life.21
Smiths (Sydney) Moral Philosophy. 21
"(G. V.) Assyrian Prophecies. 21 (G.) Wesleyan Methodism. 21 (J.) Shipwreck of
St. Paul. 21
Southeys Life of Wesley. 21
Stephens Ecclesiastical Biography. 22
Taylors Loyola 22
Wesley. 22
Theologia Germanica. 7
Thumb Bible (The). 22
Turners Sacred History. 23
Youngs Christ of History. 24
Mystery 24
Poetry and the Drama.

Aikins (Dr.) British Poets. 5

Arnolds Merope 5

"Poems 5

Baillies (Joanna) Poetical Works. 5

Calverts Wifes Manual. 8

Goldsmiths Poems, illustrated. 10 Horace, edited by Yonge.24

L. E. L. s Poetical Works. 13

Linwoods Anthologia Oxonieneis. 14

Lyra Germanica 7 M. t! in. iv1. Lars of Ancient Rome. 14 Macdonalds Within and Without. 15 Hawkers Young Sportsman The Hunting-Field. Idlea Hints on Shooting 11

Montgomerys Poftical Workm. 26 "Poems.14 Pocket and the Stud 10 12

Moores Poetical Works.26 Practical Horsemanship 10

"Selections (illustrated). 26 " Lslla Rookh. 17 Irish Melodies.17 " National Melodies. 17 " Sacred Songs Iwith Jfuriv). 17 " Songs and Ballads.16 Reades Poetical Works.19 Pycrofts Cricket-Field. 9

JUreys Horse-Taming. Richardsons Horsemanship Ronaldss Fly-Fishers Entomology Stable Talk and Table Talk Stonehenge on the Dog " " Greyhound Thackers Coursers Guide 19 19 20 10 22 22 22

Shakspeare, bv Bowdler. 20 Southeys Poetical Works. 21 The Stud, for Practical Purposes 10

Thomsons Seasons, illustrated. 22 Veterinary Medicine, andc,

Political Economy and Statistics. Cecips Stable Practice. " Stud Farm. 8

Macleods Political Economy.,.15 Hunting-Field (The) 10

MCullochs Geog. Statist. andc. Diet. 15 Miless Horse-Shoeing. "on the Horses Foot 26

"Dictionary of Commerce. 15 WUlichs Popular Tables. , 24 Pocket and the Stud Practical Horsemanship. 26

10 10

Rareys Horse-Taming. 19

Richardsons Horsemanship 19

The Sciences in general and Stable Talk and Table Talk Stonehenge on the Dog. 10 28

Mathematics. Stud (The) 10 24

Aragos Meteorological Essays. 5 1ouatts The Dog The Horse. 24

"Popular Astronomy.

Bourne on the Screw Propeller " "s Catechism ofsteam-Engine, Boyds Naval Cadets Manual Voyages and Travels.

Brandes Dictionary of Science, andc. Bakers Wanderings in Ceylon 5

"Lectures on Organic Chemistry Barths African Travels. 5

Cresya Civil Engineering. 8 Burtons East Africa. 7

Delioeches Geology of Cornwall andc. 9 De la Rives Electricity.9 Groves Correlation of Physical Forces. 10 Herscheps Outlines of Astronomy. 11 Hollands Mental Physiology.11 Humboldts Aspects of Nature. 12 "Medina and Mecca. Daviess Visit to Algiers. Domenechs Texas snd Mexico. Foresters Sardinia and Corsica Hinchliffs

Travels in the Alps Hewitts Art-Student in Munich. 7 9 9 10 11 12
"Cosmos.12 Hunt on Light 12 "(W.) Victoria. Hues Chinese Empire. 12 12
Larlners Cabinet Cyclopedia. 13 Hudson and Kennedys Mont Blanc 12
Marcets (Mrs.) Conversations. 15 Morells Elements of Psychology., 17 Hamboldts
Aspects of Nature. Hutchinsons Western Africa 12
Moseleys Engineering and Architecture 17 Ogilviea Master-Builders Plan. 18 Owens
Lectures on Comp. Anatomy. IS Pereira on Polarised Light. 18 Peschels Elements
of Physics 18 Phillipss Fossils of Cornwall.18 MClures North-West Passage. Mac
Dougalls Voyage of the Resolute. Osborns Quedah. 12
Scherzers Central America. Seawards Narrative. Snows Tierra del Fuego. IS 15 18
20 20 21
"Mineralogy. 18 " Guide to Geology.18 Portlocks Geology of Londonderry 18 Von
Tempskys Mexico and Guatemala Wanderings m the Land of Ham. Welds Vacations
in Ireland. 23 24
Powells tnity of Worlds.   19 " Christianity without Judaism 19 Smees Electro-
Metallurgy. 21 United States and Canada.
Steam-Engine (The). 6 "Works of Fiction.
Bural Sports. Cruikshanks Falstaff. Heirs of Cheveleigh 9
Hewitts Tallangetta Moores Epicurean. Sir Roger De Coverley. Sketches (The), Three
Tales Southeys Doctor, andc,. Trollopes Barchester Towers " Warden 11
Bakers Rifle and Hound in Ceylon 5 Blaines Dictionary of Sports., 6 Cecils Stable
Practice. 8 " Stud Farm. 8 Davys Fishing Excursions, 2 Series 9 Ephemera on An-
gling. q 12 17 21 21 21 22 22
Book of the Salmon . 9 Vrsul 20
   NEW WORKS and NEW EDITIONS
   LONGMAN, BBOWN, GREEN, LONGMANS, and ROBERTS,
   PATERNOSTER ROW, LONDON.
   Miss Actons Modern Cookery for Private Families, reduced to a System of Easy
Practice in a Series of carefully-tested Receipts, in which the Principles of Baron
Liebig and other eminent writers have been as much as possible applied and explained.
Newly-revised and enlarged Edition; with 8 Plates, comprising 27 Figures, and 150
Woodcuts. Fcp. 8vo. 7s. 6d.
   Actons English Bread-Book for
   Domestic Use, adapted to Families of every grade. Fcp. 8vo. price 4s. 6d.
   Aikins Select Works of the
   British Poets from Ben Jonson to Beattie. New Edition; with Biographical and
Critical Prefaces, and Selections from recent Poets. 8vo. 18s.
   Arago (F,)–Biographies of Distinguished Scientific Men. Translated by Admiral
W. H. Smyth, D. C. L., F. R. S., andc.; the Rev. Baden Powell, M. A.; and Roeert
Grakt, M. A., F. R. A. S. 8vo. 18s.
   Aragos Meteorological Essays. With an Introduction by Baron Hum- Eoldt. Trans-
lated under the superintendence of Lient.-Col. E. Saeine, R. A., Treasurer and V. P.
R. S. 8vo. 18s.
   Aragos Popular Astronomy.

Translated and edited by Admiral W. H. Smyth, D. C. L. F. R. S.; and Ro Eert Grant, M. A., F. R. A. S. In Two Volumes. Vol. I. 8vo. with Plates and Woodcuts,21s.– Vol. II. is in the press.

Arnold.–Merope, a Tragedy. By Matthew Arnold. With a Preface and an Historical Introduction. Fcp. 8vo. 5s.

Arnold.–Poems. By Matthew Arnold. First Series, Third Edition. Fcp. 8vo. 5s. 6d. Second Series, price 5s.

Lord Bacons Works. A New

Edition, collected and edited by R. L. Ellis, M. A., Fellow of Trinity College, Cambridge; J. Spedding. M. A. of Trinity College, Cambridge; and D. D. Hhath, Esq., Barrieter-at-Law, and late Fellow of Trinity College, Cambridge. Vols I. to III. 8vo. 18s. each: Vol. IV. 14s.; and Vol. V. 18s. comprising the Division of Philosophical Wandrfca; with a copious Index.

Vols. VI. and VII. comprise Bacons Literary and Professional Works. Vol. VI. price 18s. now ready.

Joanna Baillies Dramatic and

Poetical Works: Comprislnqfflays of the Passions, Miscelisneous rjramas, Metrical Legends, Fugitive Pieces, and Ahalya Baee; with the Life of Joanna Baillie, Portrait and Vignette. Square crown 8vo. 21s. cloth; or42s. morocco.

Baker.–The Rifle and the Hound in Ceylon. By S. W. Baker, Esq. New Edition, with 13 Illustrations engraved on Wood. Fcp. 8vo. 4s. 6d.

Baker.–Eight Years Wanderings in Ceylon. By S. W. Baker, Esq. With 6 coloured Plates. 8vo. 15s.

Earth.–Travels and Discoveries in North and Central Africa: Beingthe Journal of an Expedition undertaken under the auspices of Her Britannic Majestys Government in the Years ISM–1855. By Heneybarth, Ph. D., D. C. L., andc. With numerous Maps and Illustrations. 5 vols. 8vo. 5. 5s. cloth.

Bayldons Art of Valuing Rents and Tillages, and Claims of Tenants upon Quitting Farms, at both Michaelmas and Lady-day; as revised by Mr. Donaldson. Seventh Edition, enlarged and adapted to the Present Time. By Roeert Baker, Land-Agent and valuer. 8vo. price 10s. 6d.

Blacks Practical Treatise on

Brewing, based on Chemical and Economical Principles: With Formulae for Public Brewers, and Instructions for Private Families. 8vo. 10s. 6d.

Elaines Encyclopedia of Rural Sports: or, a complete Account, Historical, Practical, and Descriptive, of Hunting, Shooting, Fishing, Racing, andc. New Edition, revised and corrected to the Present Time; with above 000 Woodcut Illustrations, including 20 Subjects now added from Designs by John Leech.

Blairs Chronological and Historical Tables, from the Creation to the Present Time: With Additions and Corrections from the most authentic Writers; including the Computation of St. Paul, as connecting the Period from the Exode to the Temple. Under the revision of Sir Henky Ellis, K. H. Imperial 8vo. 31s. 6d. half-morocco.

Boyd.–A Manual for Naval

Cadets. Published with the sanction and approval of the Lords Commis-sionen of the Admiralty. By John MNJRL Boyd, Captain, R. N. With Compass-Signals in Colours, and 236 Woodcuts. Fcp. 8vo. 10s. 6d.

Bloomfield.–The Greek Testa.

ment: with copious English Notes, Critical, Philological, and Explanatory. Espe-cially adapted to the use of Theological Students and Ministers. By the Rev. 8. T. Bloompield, D. D., F. S. A. Ninth Edition, revised. 2 vols. 8vo. with Map, 2.8s.

Dr. Bloomfiolds College and School

Edition of the Greek Testament: With brief English Notes, chiefly Philological and Explanatory. Seventh Edition; with Map and Index. Fcp. 8vo. 7s. 6d.

Dr. Bloomfields College and School

Lexicon to the Greek Testament. New Edition, revised. Fcp. 8vo. price 10s. 6d.

Bournes Catechism of the Steam

Engine in its various Applications to Mines, Mills, Steam Navigation, Railways, and Agriculture: With Practical Instructions for the Manufacture and Management of Engines of every class. Fourth Edition, enlarged; with 89 Woodcuts. Fcp. 8vo. 6s.

Bourne.–A Treatise on the

Steam Engine, in its Application to Mines, Mills, Steam Navigation, and Railways. By the Artisan Club. Edited by John Boukne, C. E. New Edition; with 33 Steel Plates, and 349 Wood Engravings. 4to. 27s.

Bourne.–A Treatise on the

Screw Propeller: With various Suggestions of Improvement. By Johit Bourne, C. E. New Edition, with 20 large Plates and numerous Wood

Engravings. 4to. 38s.

Brandos Dictionary of Science,

Literature, and Art; comprising the History, Description, and Scientific Principles of every Branch of Human Knowledge; with the Derivation and Definition of all the Terms hi general use. Third Edition, revised and corrected; withnumerouswoodcuts. 8vo.60s.

Professor Brandes Lectures on

Organic Chemistry, as applied to Manufactures, including Dyeing, Bleaching, Calico Printing, Sugar Manufacture, the Preservation of Wood, Tanning, andc. Edited by J. Scoffeen", MJi. Fcp. Woodcuts, 7s. 6d.

Brewer.–An Atlas of History and Ge()graphy, from the Commencement of the Christian Era to the Present Time: Comprising a Series of Sixteen Coloured Maps, arranged in Chronological Order, with Illustrative Memoirs. By the Rev. J. S. Beewee, M. A. Second Edition, revised and corrected. Royal 8vo. 12s. 6d. half-bound.

Brialmont.–The Life of the

Duke of Wellington. From the French of Alexis Brialmont, Captain on the Staff of the Belgian Army: Withemen-dations and Additions. By the Rev. G. R. Gleig, M. A., Chaplain-General to the Forces and Prebendary of St. Pauls. With Maps, Plans, and Portraits. Vols. I. and II. 8vo. price 80s. Vol. III. (completion) is in preparation.

Dr. T. Bulls Hints to Mothers on the Management of their Health during the Period of Pregnancy and in the Lying-in Room: With an Exposure of Popular Errors in connexion with those subjects, andc.; and Hints upon Nursing. New Edition. Fcp. 8vo. 5s.

Bull.–The Maternal Management of Children in Health and Disease. By T. Bull, M. D., formerly Physician-Accoucheur to the Finsbury Midwifery Institution. New Edition. Fcp. 8vo. 5s.

Brodie.–Psychological Inqui ries, in a Series of Essays intended to illustrate the Influence of the Physical Organisation on the Mental Faculties. By Sir Benjamin C. Brodie, Bart. Third Edition. Fcp.8vo.6s.

Bunsen.–Christianity and Mankind, their Beginnings and Prospects. By Baion C. C. J. BimskN, D. D., D. C. L., D. Ph. Being a New Edition, corrected, re-modelled, and extended, of Hippolytus and, Aw Aye. 1 vols. 3vo. 5. 5s., This Edition Ib composed of three dis tinct work, as follows:– 1. Hippolytua and his Age; or, the Beginnings and Prospects of Christianity. 2 vols. 8ro. 1. i ",.

2. Outline of the Philosophy of Universal History applied to Language and Reli- gion; containing an Account of the Alphabetical Conferences. 2 vols. 33, 3. Analecta Ante-Nicna. 3 vols. Svo. 2. 2s.

Bnnsen.–Lyra Germanica.

Translated from the German by Cathe Rine Winkwoeth. Fifth Edition of the Fikst Si: f(ir, Hymns for the Sundays and Festivals of the Christian Year. Second Series, the Christian Life. Fcp. 8vo. 5s. each Series.

"," Tbese selections of German Hymns have been made from collections published in Ger-muiy by Baron Bun Sen ; and form companion volumea to

Theologia Germanica: Which setteth forth many fair lineaments of Divine Truth, and saith very lofty and lovely things touching a Perfect Life. Translated by Susanna Winkwoeth. With a Preface by the Rev. Charles Kingsley ; and a Letter by Baron X. Third Edition. Fcp.8vo.5s.

Bunsen,–Egypts Place in Uni versal History: An Historical Investigation, in Five Books. By Baron C. C. J. BunSBN, D. C. L., D. Ph. Translated from the German by C. H. Cottrell, Esq., M. A. With many Illustrations. Vol. I. 8vo. 28s.; Vot. II. 8vo. 30s. Vots. III. IV. and V. completing the work, are in the press.

Bishop Butlers Sketch of Mo dern and Ancient Geography. New Edition, thor- oughly revised, with such Alterations introduced as continually progressive Discov- eries and the latest Information have rendered necessary. Post 8vo. 7s. 6d.

Bishop Butlers General Atlas of Modern ami Ancient Geography; comprising Fifty-two full-coloured Maps; with complete Indices. New Edition, enlarged, and greatly improved. Edited by the Authors Son. Royal 4to. 24s.

Burton.–First Footsteps in East

Africa; or, an Exploration of Harar. By Richard F. Hdeton, Captain. Bombay Army. With Maps and coloured Plate. 8vo. 18s.

Burton.–Personal Narrative of a Pilgrimage toelmedinahandmeceah. By Richard F. Burton, Captain, Bombay Army. Second Edition, revised; with coloured Plates and Woodcuts. 2 vols. crown 8vo.24a.

The Cabinet Lawyer: A Popular Digest of the Laws of England, Civil and Criminal: with a Dictionary of Law Terms, Maxims, Statutes, and Judicial Antiquities; Correct Tables of Assessed Taxes, Stamp Duties, Excise Licenses, and Post-Horse Duties;

Post-Office Regulations; and Prison. Discipline. 17th Edition, comprising the Public Acts of the Session 1858. Fcp. 8vo. 10s. 6d.

The Cabinet Gazetteer: A Popular Exposition of All the Countries of the World. By the Author of The Cabinet Lawyer. Fcp. 8vo. 10s. 6d.

Calendars of State Papers, Domestic Series, published under the Direction of the Master of the Rolls, and with the Sanction of U. M. Secretary of State for the Home Department:

The Reign of JAMES 1.1603-23, edited by Mrs. Green. Vols. I. to III, imperial 8vo. 15s. each.

The Reian of CHARLES I. 1625-26, edited by Jomr Beuce, V. P. S. A. Imperial 8vo. 15e.

The Reigns of EDWARD VI., MARY, ELIZABETH, 1517-80, edited by R. Lemon, Esq. Imperial 8vo. 15s.

Historical Notes relative to the History of England, from the Accession of HENRY VIII. to the Death of ANNE (1509-1714), compiled by F. S. Thomas, Esq. 3 vols. imperial 8vo. 40fi.

State Papers relating to SCOTLAND, from the Reign of HENRY VIII. to the Accession of JAMES I. (1509-1603), and of the Correspondence relating to MARY QUEEN of-SCOTS, durinc her Captivity in England, edited by M. J. Thohpe, Esq. 2 vols. imperial 8vo. 30a.

Culvert.–The Wifes Manual; or, Prayers, Thoughts, and Songs on Several Occasions of a Matrons Life. By the Rev. W. Cilvibt, M. A. Ornamented from Designs by the Author in the style of Quten Elizabeth Prayer Book. Crown 8vo. 10s. 6d.

Catlows Popular Concliology; or, the Shell Cabinet arranged according to the Modern System: With " detailed Account of the Animals, and complete Descriptive List of the Families and Genera of Recent and Fossi Shells. Second Edition, improved; with 405 Woodcuts. Post 8vo. 11s.

Cecil.–The Stud Farm; or,

Hints on Breeding Horses for the Turf, the Chase, and the Road. Addressed to Breeders of Race-Horses and Hunters, Landed Proprietors, and Tenant Farmers. By Cecil. Fcp. 8vo. 5s.

Cecils Stable Practice; or, Hints on Training for the Turf, the Chase, and the Road; with Observations on Racing and Hunting, Wasting, Race-Riding, and Handicapping: Addressed to all who are concerned in Racing, Steeple-Chasing, and Fox-Hunting. Fcp, avo. with Plate, 5s.

Chronicles and Memorials of

Great Britain and Ireland during the Middle Ages, published by the authority of H. 51. Treasury under the Direction of the Master of the Rolls:–Capgraves Chronicle of England. edited by the Rev. F. C. Hnfeesroir, M. A.

Royal 8vo. 8s. 6d.

Chronieon Monasterii de Abingdon, edited by the Rev. J. Stevenson, M. A. Vol. I. royal 8vo. 8s. 6d.

Lives of Edward the Confessor, edited by the Rev. H. R. Ldaed, M. A. 8s. 6d.

Monumenta Franciscana, edited by the Rev. J. S. Beewee, M. A. 8s. 6d.

Fasciculi Zizaniorum Magistri Johan-nis Wyclif cum Tritico, edited by the Rev. W. W. Sbieley, M. A. 8s. d.

Stewarts Bulk of the Cronielis of Scotland, edited by W. B. Tuenbull Barrister. Vol. I. royal 8vo. 8s. 6d.

Johannis Capgrave Liber de Illustribus Henrias, edited by the Rev. F. C. HntgEstOir, M. A. Royal 8vo. 8s. 6d.

English Translation of Capgraves Boot? f ttejUuttrimu Henries, by the Rev. F. C. Hingeston, M. A. 10s. 6d.

Elmhams Historia de Monasterii S. Augustim Cantuarensis, edited by the Rev. C. HibDwicKE, M. A. 8s 6d

Chapman.–History of Gustavus Adolphus, and of the Thirtv Years War up to the Kings Death: With some Account of its Conclusion by the Peace of Westphalia, in 1648. By B. t l 1 . m Im N , M. A. 8vo. Plans, 12s. 6d.

Chevreul On the Harmony and neror ecoraon, apesres, ar pets, Mosaics, Coloured Glazing, Paper-Staining, Cabco-Printing, Letterpress-Printing, Map-Colouring, Dress, Landscape and Flower-Gardening, andc. andc. Translated by Chables Maetel. With I Plates. Crown 8vo. 10s. 6d.

Connolly.–History of the Royal Sappers and Miners: Including the Services of the Corps in the Crimea and at the Siege of Sebastopol. By T. W. J. Cojnf Oll Y, Quartermaster of the Royal Engineers. Second Edition; with 17 coloured Plates, 2 vols. 8vo. 80s.

Conybeare and Howsoiis Life and Epistles of Saint Paul: Comprising a complete Biography of the Apostle, and a Translation of his Epistles inserted in Chronological Order. Third Edition, revised and corrected; with several Maps and Woodcuts, and 4 Plates. 2 vols. square crown 8vo. 31s. 6d. " The Original Edition, with more nu merous Illustrations, in 2 vols. 4to. price 48s.

–may also be had.

Dr. Coplands Dictionary of

Practical Medicine: Comprising General Pathology, the Nature and Treatment of Diseases, Morbid Structures, and the Disorders especially incidental to Climates, to Sex, and to the different Epochs of Life; with numerous approved Formulte of the Medicines recommended. Now complete in 3 vols. 8vo. price 5. lls. cloth.

Bishop Cottons Instructions in the Doctrine and Practice of Christianity. Intended as an Introduction to Confirmation. 4th Edition. 18mo.2s. 6d.

Cresys Encyclopaedia of Civil

Engineering, Historical, Theoretical, ana Practical. Illustrated by upwards of 3,000 Woodcuts. Seeona Edition, revised; and extended in a Supplement comprising Metropolitan Water-supply, Drainage of Towns, Railways, Cubical Proportion, Brick and Iron Construction, Iron Screw Piles, Tubular Bridges andc. 8vo. 63s.

Crosse.–Memorials, Scientific and Literary, of Andrew Crosse, the Electrician. Edited by Mrs. Ceosse. Post 8vo. 9s. 6d.

Crowe.–The History of France.

By Eyee Evans Crowe. In Five Volumes. Vol. I. 8vo. 14s.

Cruikshank.–The Life of Sir

John Falstaff. illustrated in a Series of Twenty-foul-original Etchings by George Cruikshank. Accompanied by an imaginary Biography of the Knight, by Roeeet 13. Brocgh. Royal 8vo, price 12s. 6d. cloth.

Lady Custs Invalids Own Book: A Collection of Recipes from various Books and various Countries. Second Edition. Fcp. 8vo. 2s. 6d.

The Rev. Canon Dales Domestic

Liturgy and Family Chaplain, in Two Parts: Part I. Churchservices adapted for Domestic Use, with Prayers for Every Day of the VVeek, selected from the Book of Common Prayer; Paet II. an appropriate Sermon for Every Sunday in the Year. Second Edition. Post 4to. 21s. cloth; 31s. (3d. calf; or 2.10s. morocco.

, The Famu. t Chaplain, 12s. Separately The Domestic Liturgi, I 10s. 6ci.

Davies.–Algiers in 1857: Its

Accessibility, Climate, and Resources described with especial reference to English Invalids; with details of Recreation obtainable in its Neighbourhood added for the use of Travellers in general. By the Rev. E. W. L. Davies, M. A. Oxon. Post Svo. 6s.

Delabeche.–Report on the Geology of Cornwall, Devon, and West Sqmerset. By Sir H. T. Delaeeche, F. R. S. With Maps, Plates, and Woodcuts. 8vo. 14s.

Davy (Dr. J.)–The Angler and his Friend; or, Piscatory Colloquies and Fishing Excursions. By Johlr Davy, M. D., F. R. S., to. Fcp. 8vo. 6s.

By the same Author,

The Angler in the Lake District; or, Piscatory Colloquies and Fishing Excursions in Westmoreland and Cumberland. Fcp. 8vo. 6s. 6d,

De la Rives Treatise on Elec- t ricity in Theory and Practice. Translated for the Author by C. V. Walker, F. B. S. 3 vols.8vo. Woodcuts, 3.13s.

Abbe Domenechs Missionary

Adventures in Texas and Mexico: A Personal Narrative of Six Years Sojourn in those Regions. Translated from the French uuder the Authors superintendence. 8vo. 10s. 6d.

The Eclipse of Faith; or, a Visit to a Religious Sceptic. th Edition. Fcp. 8vo. as.

Defence of The Eclipse of Faith, by its Author: Being a Rejoinder to Professor Newmans Reply: Including a full Examination of that Writers Criticism on the Character of Christ; and a Chapter on the Aspects and Pretensions of Modern Deism. Second Edition, revised. Post 8vo. 5s. 6d.

The Englishmans Greek Concordance of the New Testament: Being an Attempt at a Verbal Connexion between the Greek and the English Texts; including a Concordance to the Proper Names, with Indexes, Greek-English and English-Greek. New Edition, with a new Index. Koyal 8vo. 42s.

The Englishmans Hebrew and

Chaldee Concordance of the Old Testament: Being an Attempt at a Verbal Connexion between the Original and the English Translations; with Indexes, a List of the Proper Names and their Occurrences, andc. 2 vols. royal 8vo. S. 13s. 6d.; large paper, 4.14s. 6d.

Ephemerashandbookofangling; teacliing Fly-fishing, Trolling, Bottom-Fishing, Salmon-Fishing: With the Natural History of Kiver-Fish, and the best Modes of

Catching them. Third Edition, corrected and improved; with Woodcuts. Fcp. 8vo. 5s.

Ephemeras Book of the Salmon: The Theory, Principles, and Practice of Fly-Fishing for Salinou; Lists of good Salmon Flies for every good River in the Empire; the Natural History of the Salmon, its Habits described, and the best way of artificially Breeding it. Fcp. 8vo, with coloured Plates, 14s.

Fairbairn.–Useful Information for Engineers: Being a Series of Lectures delivered to the Working Engineers of Yorkshire and Lancashire. By William Faieeaien, F. R. S., F. G. S. Second Edition; with Plates and Woodcuts. Crown 8vo. lys. 6d.

Fischer.–Francis Bacon of

Verulam: Realistic Philosophy and its Age. By Dr. K. Fischeb. Translated by John OxesroeU. Post 8vo. 9s. 6d.

Forester.–Rambles in the Islands of Corsica and Sardinia: With Notices of their History, Antiquities, and present Condition. By Tiiomas Forbstkr. With coloured Map; and numerous Lithographic and Woodcut Illustrations from Drawings made during the Tom-by Lieut-Col. M. A. Biddulph, R. A. Imperial 8vo. 28s.

Garratt.–Marvels and Mysteries of Instinct; or, Curiosities of Animal Life. By Geobge Oabbatt. Second Edition, improved. Fcp. 8vo.4s. 6d.

Gillian.–A Practical Treatise on Banking. By James William Ollbabt, F. R. S., General Manager of the London and Westminister Bank. Sixth Edition. 2 vols. I2mo. 16s.

Gilbart.–Logic for the Million: a Familiar Exposition of the Art of Reasoning, Byj. W. Gilbabt, F. R. S. 5thedition; with Portrait. 12mo.3s.6d.

Oleig.–Essays, Biographical,

Historical, and Miscellaneous, contributed chiefly to the Edinburgh and Quarterly Beviews. By the Rev. G. R. Gleig, M. A., Chaplain-General to the Forces, and Prebendary of St. Pauls. 2 vols. 8vo. price 21s.

The Poetical Work of Oliver

Goldsmith. Edited by Bolton Cobney, Esq. Illustrated by Wood Engravings, from Designs by Members of the Etching Club. Square crown 8vo. cloth, 2is.; morocco, 1.16s.

Gpsse.–A Naturalists Sojourn in Jamaica. By P. H. G08SE, Esq. With Plates. Post 8vo. Us.

Greathed.–Letters from Delhi during the Siege. Byh. H. Gbbathed Esq., Political Agent. Post 8vo.

Green.–Lives of the Princesses of England. By Mrs. Maby An"ne Evebett Gbeen, Editor of the Letters of Royal ami Illustrious Ladies. With numerous Portraits. Complete in 6 vols. post 8vo. 10s. 6d, each.

Greyson.–Selections from" the Correspondence of R. E. Gbkyson, Esq. Edited by the Author of The 2clip, e of faith. New Edition. Crown 8vo. 7s. 6d.

Grove.–The Correlation of Physical Forces. By W. R. Gbove, O. C M. A. TMra Edition. 8vo. 7s.

Gurney.–St. Louis and Henri
IV.: Being a Second Series of Histo-

rical Sketches. By the Rev. John H.
Guwmr, M. A. Fcp. 8vo. 6.

Eveningbecreations; or, Samples
from the Lecture-Room. Edited by
Rev. J. H. Gubney. Crown 8vo. 5s.

Gwilts Encyclopedia of Architecture, Historical, Theoretical, and Practical. By
Joseph Gwilt. With more than1,000 Wood Engravings, from Designs by J. S. Gwilt.
8vo. 42s.

Hare (Archdeacon).–The Life of Luther, in Forty-eight Historical Engravings. By
Guhtav Koxig. With Explanations by Archdeacon Habe and ScsaHifih Winewobih.
Fcp. 4to. 28s.

Harford.–Life of Michaelangelo
Buonarroti: With Translations of many of his Poems and Letters: also Memoirs
of Savonarola, Raphael, and Vittoriacolonna. By Johits. HABFOBD, Esq., D. C.
L., F. R. S. Second Edition, revised; with20 Plates. 2vols.8vo.25s., Illustrations,
Architectural and

Pictorical, of the Genius of Michael
Angelo Buonarroti. With Descriptions
of the Plates, by the Commendatore
CANlnA; C. R. Cockebbli,, Esq R. A.;
and J. S. Habeobd. Esq., D. C. L., F. H. S.
Folio, 73s. 6d. half-bound.

Harrison.–The Light of the
Forge; or. Counsels from the Sick-Bed
of KM. By the Rev. W. Habbison",
M. A., Domestic Chaplain to the
Duchess of Cambridge. Fcp. Svo. 5s. i

Harry Hieovers Stable Talk
and Tahle Talk; or. Spectacles for
Young Sportsmen. New Edition, 2
vols. 8vo. Portrait, 24s.

Harry Hieover.–The Hunting-Field. By Haeby Hieotib. With. Two Plates. Fcp.
8vo. 5s. half-bound.

Harry Hieover.–Practical Horsemanship. Second Edition; with 2 Plates. Fcp. 8vo.
5s. half-bound.

Harry Hieover.–The Pocket and the Stud; or, Practical Hints on the
M anagement of the Stable. By H A u u v Hieoveb. Fcp. 8vo. Portrait, 5s.

Harry Hieover.–The Stud, for Practical Purposes and Practical Men: Being a Guide
to the Choice of a Horse for use more than for show. Fcp. 5s.

Kassall.–A History of the British Freshwater Algffi: Including Descriptions of the
Desmidess and Diatomacese. By Abthub Hill Has- Sall, M. D. 2 vols. 8vo. with 103
Plates, 1.15s.

Hassall.–Adulterations Detected; or, Plain Instructions for the Dis co-very of Frauds
in Food and Medicine. By Abthub Hill Has all, M. D. Lond., Analyst of The Lancet
Sanitary Commission, and Author of the Reports of that Commission published under

the title of Food and its Adulterations (which may also be had, in 8vo. price 28s.) With 225 Illustrations, engraved on Wood. Crown 8vo. 17s. 6d.

Col. Hawkers Instructions to Young Sportsmen in all that relates to Guns and Shooting. 10th Edition, revised by the Authors Son, Major P. W. l. haweeb. With Portrait, Plates, and Woodcuts. 8vo. 21s.

Haydns Book of Dignities:

Containing Rolls of the Official Personages of the British Empire, Civil, Ecclesiastical, Judicial, Military, Naval, and Municipal, from the Earliest Periods to the Present Time. Together with the Sovereigns of Europe, from the Foundation of their respective States; the Peerage and Nobility of Great Britain, andc. 8vo. 25s.

Hayward.–Biographical and

Critical Essays, reprinted from Reviews, with Additions and Corrections. By A. Haywabd, Esq., Q. C. 2 vols. 8vo. 24s.

The Heirs of Cheveleigh: A

Novel. By Geevaise Abbott. 3 vols. post 8vo. 31s. 6d.

Sir John Herschels Outlines of

Astronomy. Fifth Edition, revised and corrected to the existing state of astronomical knowledge; with Plates and Woodcuts. 8vo. 18s.

Sir John Herschels Essays from the Edinburgh and Quarterly Reviews, with Addresses and other Pieces, 8vo. 18s.

Hinchliff.–Summer Months among the Alps: With the Ascent of Monte Rosa. BytHOs. W. HlnCHLlfF, Barrister-at-Law. Post 8vo. 10s. 6d.

Hints on Etiquette and the

Usages of Society: With a Glance at

Bad Habits. New Edition, revised

(with Additions) by a Lady of Rank

Fcp. 8vo. 2s. 6d.

Holland.–Medical Notes and

Reflections. By Sir Henby Holland.

M. D., F. R. S., andc., Physician in Ordil

nary to the Queen and Prince-Consort.

Third Edition. 8vo. 18s.

Holland.–Chapters on Mental

Physiology. By Sir Henby HoltimD,

Bart., F. R. S., andc. Founded chiefly on

Chapters contained in Medical Notes

and Reflectiont by the same Author.

Second Edition. Post 8vo. 8s. 6d.

Hooker.–Kew Gardens; or, a

Popular Guide to the Royal Botanic Gardens of Kew. By Sir William Jaceson" Hooeeb, K. H., andc Director. With many Woodcuts. 16mo. 6d.

Hookers Museum of Economic

Botany; or, Popular Guide to the Useful and Remarkable Vegetable Products of the Museum in the Royal Gardens of Kew. 16mo. Is.

Hooker and Arnotts British j

Flora; comprising the Phcenogamous or Flowering Plants and the Ferns. Seventh Edition, with Additions and Corrections; and numerous Figures illustrative of the Umbelliferous Plants the Composite Plants, the Grasses, and the Ferns. 12mo. with 12 Plates. Ms. with the Plates coloured, 21s.

Homes Introduction to the

Critical Study and Knowledge of the Holy Scriptures. Tenth Edition, revised, corrected, and brought down to the present time. Edited by the Rev. T. Habtwell Hobnb. B. D. (the Author); the Rev. Samuil Davidson, D. D. of the University of Halle, ancl LL. D.; and S. Peideaux Tieohlles, LL. D. With 4 Maps and 22 Vignettes and Facsimiles. 4 vols. 8vo. 3.13s. 6d.

Home.–A Compendious Introduction to the Study of the Bible. By the Rev. T. Habtwell Hobne, B. D. New Edition, with Maps, ando. 12mo. 9s.

Hoskyns.–Talpa; or, the Chronicles of a Clay Farm: An gricullural Fragment. By Chalfois Wben Hoseyns, Esq. Fourth Ediinn. With 24 Woodcuts from Designs by Geobgb Ceuieshane. 16mo. 5s. 6d.

How to Nurse Sick Children: Intended especially as a Help to the Nurses in the Hospital for Sick Children; bnt containing Directions of service to all who have the charge of the Yonng. Fcp. 8vo. Is. 6d.

Howitt (A. H.)–An Art-Student in Munich. By AwnA Maey Howrit. 2 vols. post 8vo. 14s.

Howitt.–The Childrens Tear.

By Mary Howitt. With Four Illustrations. Square 16mo. 5s.

Howitt.–Tallangetta, the

Squatters Home: A Story of Australian Life. By William Howirr. 2 vols. post 8vo. 18s.

Howitt.–Land, Labour, and

Gold; or, Two Years in Victoria: With Visit to Sydney and Van Diemens Land. By William Howitt. Second

Edition. 2 vols. crown 8vo. 10s.

W. Howittsvisits toremarkable Places: Old Halls, Battle-Fields, and Scenes il-lustrative of Striking Passages in English History and Poetry. With about 80 Wood Engravings. New Edition. 2 vols. square crown 8vo. 25s.

William Howitts Boys Country Book: Being the Real Life of a Country Boy, written by himself; exhibiting all the Amusements, Pleasures, and Pursuits of Children in the Country. With 40 Woodcuts. Fcp. 8vo. 6s.

William Howitts Rural Life of

England. With Woodcuts by Bewick and Williams. Medium 8vo. 21s.

Hue.–Christianity in China, Tartary, and Thibet. By M.

Hue, formerly Missionary Apostolic China. Vols. I. and II. 8vo. 21s.; and Vol. Ill 10s. 6d.

Hue.–The Chinese Empire:

A Sequel to Hue and Gabets Journey through Tartaryand Thibet. By the Abbe Hue, formerly Missionary Apostolic in China. Secotul Edition; with Map. 2 vols. 8vo. 24s.

Hudson and Kennedys Ascent of Mont Blanc by a New Route and Without Guides. Second Edition, with Plate and Map. Post 8vo. 5s. 6d.

Hudsons Plain Directions for
Making Wills in conformity with the
Law: With a clear Exposition of the
Law relating to the distribution of
Personal Estate in the case of Intes-
tacy, two Forms of Wills, and much
useful information. Fcp. SVo. 2s. 6d.

Hudsons Executors Guide.!
New and improved Edition; with the
Statutes enacted, and the Judicial
Decisions pronounced since the last
Edition incorporated. Fcp. 8vo. 6s.

Humboldts Cosmos. Translated, with the Authors authority, by Mrs. Saei. ve. Vols. I. and II. 16mo. Half-a-Cro wn each, sewed; 3s. 6d. each, cloth; or in post 8vo. 12s. each, cloth. Vol. III. post 8vo. 12s. 6d. cloth: or in 16mo. Part I. 2s. 6d. sewed, 3s. 6d. cloth; and Part II. 3s. sewed, 4s. cloth. Vol. IV. Paet I. post 8vo. 15s. cloth: 16mo. 7s. 6d. cloth.

Humboldts Aspects of Nature Translated, with the Authors authority, by Mrs. Saeise. 16mo. price 6s.: or in 2 vols. 3s. 6(1. each, cloth; 2s. 6d. each, sewed.

Humphreys.–Parables of Our
Lord, illuminated and ornamented in the style of the Missals of the Renaissance by H. N. Hukphreys. Square fcp. 8vo. 21s. in massive carved covers; or 30s. bound in morocco, by Hayday.

Hunt.–Researches on Light in its Chemical Relstions; embracing a Consideration of all the Photographic Processes. By Robert Hunt, F. R. S. Second Edition, with Plate and Woodcuts. 8vo. 10s. 6d.

Hutchinson.–Impressions of
Western Africa: With a Report on the Peculiarities of Trade up the Rivers in the Bight of Biafra. liyj. T. Hctchin- Sok, Esq., British Consul for the Bight of Biafra and the Island of Fernando Po. Post 8vo. 8s. 6d.

Idle.–Hints on Shooting, Fishing andc., both on Sea and Land, and in the Fresh-Water Lochs of Scotland: Being the Experiences of C. Idle, Esq. Fcp. Svo. 5s.

Mrs. Jamesons Legends of the
Saints and Martyrs, as represented in Christian Art: Forming the First Series of Sacred and Legendary Art. Third Edition; with 17 Etchings and upwards of 180 Woodcuts. 2 vols. square crown 8vo. 31s. 6d.

Mrs. Jamesons Legends of the
Monastic Orders, as represented in Christian Art. Forming the Second Sebies of Sacred and Legendary Art. Second Edition, enlarged; with 11 Etchings by the Author and 88 Woodcuts, Square crown 8vo. 28s,

Mrs. Jamesons Legends of the

Madonna, as represented in Christian Art: Forming the Thibd Sebies of Sacred and Legendary Art. Second Edition, corrected and enlarged; with 27 Etclnngs and 165 Wood Engravings, Square crown 8vo. 28s.

Sirs. Jamesons Commonplace-
Book of Thoughts, Memories, and Fancies, Original and Selected. Second Edition, revised and coriected; with Etchings and Woodcuts. Crown 8vo. price 18s.

Mrs. Jamesons Two Lectures on the Employment of Women:– 1. Sistehs of Cbahity, Catholic and Pro- testant, Abroad and at Home. Second Edition, with new Preface. Fcp. 8 o, 4s.

2. The Cowmunion of Laboub: A Second
Lecture on the Social Employments of
Women. Fcp. 8vo. 3.

Jaqucmets Compendium of Chronology: Containing the most important Dates of General History, Political, Ecclesiastical, and Literary, from the Creation of the World to the end of the Year 1854. Post 8vo. 7s. 6d.

Jiiquemcts Chronology for
Schools: Containing the most important Dates of General History, Political, Ecclesiastical, and Literary, from the Creation of the World to the eud of the Year 1857. Fcp. 8vo. 8s. 6d.

Lord Jeffreys Contributions to
The Edinburgh Review. A New Edition, complete in One Volume, with Portrait and Vignette. Square crown 8vo. 21s. cloth; or 80s. calf.–Or iu 3 vols. 8vo. price 42s.

Bishop Jeremy Taylors Entire
Works: With Life by Bishop Hbbeb. Revised and corrected by the Rev. Chables Page Eden, Fellow of Oriel College, Oxford. Now complete in 10 vols. 8vo. 10s. 6d. each.

Kemhle.–The Saxons in England: A History of the English Commonwealth till the Conquest. By J. M. Kemble, M. A. 2 vols.8vo. 28s.

Keith Johnstons Dictionary of
Geography, Descriptive. Physical, Statistical, and Historical: Forming a complete General Gazetteer of the World. Second Edition, thoroughly revised. In 1 vol. of 1,360 pages, comprising about 50,000 Names of Places, 8vo. 36s. cloth; or half-bound in russia, 41s.

Kesteven.–A Manual of the
Domestic Practice of Medicine. By W. B. Kesteven, F. R. C. S. E., andc. Square post 8vo. 7s. 6d.

Kirhy and Spences Introduction to Entomology; or, Elements of the Natural History of Insects: Comprising an Account of Noxious and Useful Insects, of their Metamorphoses, Food, Stratagems, Habitations. Societies, Motions, Noises, Hibernation, Instinct, andc. Seventh Editionf with an Appendix relative to the Origin and Progress of the work. Crown 8vo. 5s.

Lardners Cabinet Cyclopaedia of
History, Biography, Literature, the Arts and Sciences, Natural History, and Manufactures. A Series of Original Works by Eminent Wbitebs. Complete in 132 vols.

fcp. 8vo. with Vignette Titles, price 19. 19s. cloth lettered. The Works separate! y, in single Volumes or Sets, price 3s. tid. each Volume, cloth lettered.

Mrs. B. Lees Elements of Natural History; or. First Principles of Zoology: Comprising the Principles ol Classification, interspersed with amusing and instructive Accounts of the most remarkable Animals. New Edition; Woodcuts. Fcp. 8vo. 7s. 6d.

The Letters of a Betrothed.

Fcp. 8vo. price 5s. cloth.

Letters to my Unknown Friends.

By a Lady, Author of Letters on Happiness. Fourth Edition. Fcp. 8vo. 5s.

Letters on Happiness, addressed to a Friend. By the Author of Letters to my Unknown Friends. Fcp. 8vo. 6s.

L. E. L.–The Poetical Works of

Letitia Elizabeth Landon; comprising the Improvisatrice, the Venetian Bracelet, the Golden Violet, the Troubadour, and Poetical Remains. 2 vols. I6mo. 10s. cloth; morocco, 21s.

Dr. John Lindleys. Theory and

Practice of Horticulture; or, an Attempt to explain the principal Operations of Gardening upon Physiological Grounds: Being the Second Edition of the Theory of Horticulture, much enlarged; with 98 Woodcuts. Svo. 21s.

Dr. John Liudleys Introduction to Botany. New Edition, with corrections and copious Additions. 2 vols. 8vu. with Plates and Woodcuts, 24s.

Linwood.–Anthologia Oxoni- ensis, sive Florileirium e Lusibus poet-icia diverso-rum Oxoniensium Graecis et Latinis decerptum. Curante Guli- Elmo Linwood. II. A. 8vo. 14s.

Lorimers Letters to a Young Master Mariner on some Subjects connected with his Calling. Fep. 8vo. price 5s. 6d.

Londons Encyclopaedia of Gardening: Comprising the Theory and Practice of Hor-ticulture, Floriculture, Aboriculture, and Landscape-Garden-ing. With 1,000 Wood-cuts. 8vo. 50s.

Londons Encyclopaedia of Trees and Shrubs, or Aboretum et Fructice-tumbritannicumabri Containing the Hardy Trees and Shrubs of Great Britain, Native and Foreign, Scien-tifically and Popularly Described. With about 2,000 Woodcuts. 8vo. 50s.

Londons Encyclopaedia of Agriculture: Comprising the Theory and Practice of the Valuation, Transfer, Laying-out. Improvement, and Management of Landed Property, and of the Cultivation and Economy of the Animal and Vegetable Productions of Agriculture. With 1,100 Woodcuts. 8vo. 31s. 6d.

Loudons Encyclopaedia of Plants:

Comprising the Specific Character, Description, Culture, History, Application in the Arts, and every other desirable Particular respecting all the Plants found in Great Britain. With upwards of 12,000 Woodcuts. 8vo. price 3.13s, 6d.

Loudons Encyclopaedia of Cottage, Farm, and Villa Architecture and Furniture. New Edition, edited by Mrs. Loudon ; with more than 2,000 Woodcuts. 8vo. 63s.

Loudons Hortus Britannicns; or, Catalogue of all the Plants found in Great Britain. New Edition, corrected by Mrs. Loudon. 8vo.31s.6d.

Mrs. Londons Ladys Country
Companion: or. How to Enjoy a
Country Life Rationally. Fourth
Edition. Fop.8vo.9s.

Mrs. London s Amateur Gardeners Calendar, or Monthly Guide to what should be avoided and done in a Garden. Second Edition, revised. Crown 8vo. with Woodcuts, 7s. 6d.

Lows Elements of Practical
Agriculture-comprehending the Cultivation of Plants, the Husbandry of the Domestic Animals, and the Economy of the Farm. New Edition.; with 200 Woodcuts. 8vo. 21s.

Macaulay.–Speeches of the
Righthon. LordmicAtn. Ar. Corrected by Himself. 8vo. 12s.

Macaulay.–The History of
England from the Accession of James I II. By the Right Hon. Lord Mj.- I Caulay. New Edition. Vols. I. and I II. 8vo. 33s.; Vols. III. and IV. 36s.

Lord Macaulay s History of land from the Accession of James j New Edition of the first Four Volumes of the Octavo Edition, revised and corrected. 7 vols. post 8vo. 6s. each.

Lord Macaulays Critical and
Historical Essays contributed to The
Edinburgh Review. Four Editions:– 1. A Tuika Ky Edition (the Eiyhth, in 3 vols. 8vo. price 36s.

2. Complete in One Voluiu, with Por trait and Vignette-Square crown bvo. price 21s. cloth; or 30s. calf.

3. Another New Edition, in 3 vols. fcp.
Svo. price 21s. cloth.

4. The Psopijss Edition, in 2 roll.
crown 8vo. price 8s. cloth.

Macaulay.–Lays of Ancient Rome, with Ivry and the Armada. By the Right Hon. Lord Macaulay. New Edition. 16mo. price 4s. 6d. cloth; or 10s. till, bound in porocco.

Lord Macaulays Lays of Ancient
Rome. With numerous Illustrations, Original and from the Antique, drawn on Wood by George Scharf, Juk. Fcp. 4to. 21s. boards; or 42s. bound in morocco.

Mac Donald.–Poems, By George Mac Donald, Author of Within ana Without. Fcp.8vo.7s.

Mac Donald.–Within and Without: A Dramatic Poem. By
Geoege Mac Donald. Fcp, 8vo. 4s.6d.

Mac Dougall.–The Theory of
War illustrated by numerous Examples from History. By Lieutenant-Colonel Mac Dougall, Commandant of the Staff College. Second Edition, revised. Post 8vo. with Plans, 10s. 6d.

Mac Dougall.–The Campaigns of Hannibal, arranged and critically considered, expressly for the use of Students of Military History. By Lieut.-Col. P. L. Mac Dougall, Commandant of the Staff College. Post 8vo. 7s. 6d.

MDougall.–The Eventful

Voyageof H. M. Discovery Ship Resolute to the Arctic Regions in search of Sir John Franklin and the Missing Crewx of H. M. Discovery Ships Erebus and Terror, 1852,1853,1854. By George F. Mdougall, Master. With a coloured Chart, Illustrations in Lithography, and Woodcuts. 8vo. 21s.

. Sir James Mackintoshs Miscellaneous Works: Including his Contributions to The Edinburgh Review. Complete in One Volume; with Portrait and Vignette. Square crown 8vo. 21s. cloth; or 80s. hound in calf: or in 3 vols. fcp. 8vo. 21s.

Sir James Mackintoshs History of England from the Earliest Times to the final Establishment of the Reformation. 2 vols. 8vo. 21s.

Macleod.–The Elements of Political Economy. By Henky Dunming Macleod, Barrister-at-Law. 8vo. I6s.

Macleod.–The Theory and

Practice of Banking: With the Elementary Principlesof Currency, Prices, Credit, and Exchanges. By Hsirar Dunning Macleod, Barrister-at-Law. 2 vols. royal 8vo. 80s.

MCullochs Dictionary, Practical, Theoretical, and Historical, of Commerce, and Commercial Navigation. Illustrated with Maps; ind Plans. New Edition, corrected; with Supplement. 8vo. 50s. cloth; half-russia, 55s.

MCullochs Dictionary, Geographical, Statistical, and Historical. of the various Countries, Places, and principal Natural Objects in the World. Illustrated with Stelarge Maps. New Edition, revised. 2 vols. 8m 63s.

Maguire.–Home; its Ruler and itslnstitutioiis. ByjohwfRANCls Magvirk, M. P. With a Portrait of Pope Pius IX. Post 8vo. 10s. 6d.

Mrs. Murcets Conversations on

Natural Philosophy, in which the Elements of that Science are familiarly explained. Thirteenth Edition, enlarged and corrected; with 3-1 Plates. Fcp, 8vo. price 10s. 6d.

Mrs. Marcets Conversations on

Chemistry, in which the Elements of that Science are familiarly explained and illustrated by Experiments. New Edition, improved. 2vols. fcp. 8vo. 14s.

Martineau.–Studies of Christianity: A Series of Original Papers, now first collected, or New. By Jahes Maetlneau. Crown 8vo. 7s. 6d.

Martineau.–Endeavours after the Christian Life: Discourses. By James Martineau. 2 vols. post 8vo. price 7s. 6d. each.

Martineau.–Hymns for the

Christian Church and Home. Collected and edited by James Martineau. Eleventh Edition, I2mo. 3s. 6d. cloth, or 5s. calf; Fifth Edition, 32mo. Is. 4d. cloth, or ls. 8d. roan.

Martineau.–Miscellanies: Comprising Essays chiefly religious and controversial. By James Maeiiweau. Crown 8vo. 9s.

Maunders Scientific and Literary Treasury: A new and popular Encyclopedia of Science and the Belles-Lettres; including all Branches of Science, and every subject connected with Literature and Art. Fcp. Svo. 10s.

Maunders Biographical Treasury; consisting of Memoirs, Sketches, and brief Notices of above 12,000 Eminent Persons of All Ages and Nations, from the Earliest Period of History: Forming a complete Dictionary of Universal Biography. Fcp. 8vo. 10s.

Maunders Treasury of Know-ledge, and Library of Reference; comprising an English Dictionary and Grammar, a Universal Gazetteer, a Classical Dictionary, a Chronology, a Law Dictionary, a Synopsis of tli Peerage, numerous useful Tables, andc. Ftp. 8vo. 10s.

Maunderfl Treasury of Natural j History; or, a Popular Dictionary of Animated Nature: In which the Zoological Characteristics that distinguish the different Classes. Genera, and Species, are combined with a variety of interesting Information illustrative of the Habits, Instincts, and ttencr al Economy of the Animal Kingdom. With W0Woodcuts. Fcp. 10s.

Maunder s Historical Treasury;.

comprising a General Introductory

Outline of Universal History, Ancient and Modern, and a Series of Seoarat Histories of every principal Nation that exists; their Rise. Progress, and Present Condition, the Moral and Social Character of their respective Inhabitants, their Religion, Manners, and Customs, andc. Fcp. 8vo. 10s.

Maunders Treasury of Geography, Physical, Historical, Descriptive, and Political; containing a succinct Account of Every Country in the World: Preceded by an Introductory Outline of the History of Geography; a Familiar Inquiry into the arieties of Race and Language exhibited by different Nations; and a View of the Relations of Geography to Astronomy and the Physical Sciences. Completed by William Hughes. F. R. G. S. With 7 i Maps and 16 Steel Plates. Fcp. 8vo. 10s. j

Merivale.–A History of the!

Romans under the Empire. By the.

Rev. Chables Mebivale, B. D., late

Fellow of St. Johns College, Cambridge. I 8vo. with Maps.

Vols. I-and II, comprising the History to the Fall of Julius Cottar. Second Edition. 28s.

Vol. III. to the Establishment of the Monarchy by Augustus. Second Edition Ms.

Vol-. IV. and V. from Augustus to Claudius, B. c. 27 to A. D.51 32s.

Vol. VI. from the Reign of Nero, A. d. 54, to the Fall of Jerusalem, A. d. "0 16s.

Merivale.–The Fall of the

Koman Republic: A Short History of Last Century of the Com in on wealth. By the Rev. C. Mbbivale, B. D., late Fellow of St. Johns College. Cambridge. New Edition. 12mo. 7s. 6d.

Merivale (Miss).–Christian

Records: A Short History of Apostolic Anjc. By L. A. Mebivale. Fcp. 8vo. price 7s. 6d.

Miles.–The Horses Foot and

How to Keep it Sound. Eighth Edition; with an Appendixonshoeingingeneral, I and Hunters in particular. 12 Plates I and 12 Woodcuts. By W. Miles, Esq.! Imperial 8vo. 12s. 6d.

Miless Plain Treatise on Horse
Shoeing. With Plates and Woodcuts.
Second Edition. Post 8vo. 2s.

Milners History of the Church of Christ. Witli Additions by the late Rev. Isaac Milneb, D. D., F. R. S. A New Edition, revised, with additional Notes by the Rot. T. Gbamtham, B. D. 4 vols. 8vo. 52s.

James Montgomerys Poetical
Works: Collective Edition; with the Authors Autobiographical Prefaces, complete in One Volume; w ith Portrait and Vignette. Square crown 8vo. 10s. 6d. doth; morocco, 21s.–Or, in 4 vols. fcp. 8vo. with Plates, 14s.

Moore.–The Power of the Soul over the Body, considered in relation to Health, ind Morals. Uy Geobge Moobe, M. D. Fcp. 8vo. 6s.

Moore.–Man and his Motives. By Geobge Moobe, M. D. Fcp. 8vo. 6s.

Moore.–The Use of the Body in relation to the Mind. By G. Moons, M. D. Fcp. 8vo. 6s.

Moore.–Memoirs, Journal, and
Correspondence of Thomas Moore. Edited by the Right Hon. Lobd Johx Russell, M. P. With Portraits and Vignettes. 8 vols. post 8vo. 4.4s.

Thomas Moores Poetical Works:
Comprising the Authors Recent Introductions and Notes. The Travellers Edition, crown 8vo. with Portrait, 12s. 6d. cloth; morocco by Hayday, 21s.–Also the Library Edition, witu Portrait and. Vignette, medium 8vo. 21s. cloth: morocco by Hayday, 42s.–And the First collected Edition, in 10 vols. fcp.8vo. with Portrait and 19 Plates, 35s.

Moore.–Poetry and Pictures from Thomas Moore: Being Selections of the most popular and admired of Moores Poems, copiously illustrated with highly-finished Wood Engravings from original Designs by eminent Artists. Fcp. 4to. price 21s. cloth; or 42s. bound in morocco by Hayday.

Moores Songs, Ballads, and
Sacred Songs. New Edition, printed in Ruby Type; with the Notes, and a Vignette from a Design by T. Creswick, R. A. 82mo. 2s. 6d.–An Edition in 16mo. with Vignette by R-Doyle, 5s.; or 12s. 6d. morocco by Hayday.

Moores Sacred Songs, the Symphonies and Accompaniments, arranged for One or more Voices, printed with the Words. Imperial 8vo.
Nearly ready.

Moores Lalla Rookh: An Oriental Romance. With 13 highly-finished Steel Plates from Original Designs by Corbould, Meadows, and Stephanoff, engraved under the superintendence of the late Charles Heath. New Edition. Square crown 8vo. 15s. cloth; morocco, 28s.

Moores Lalla Rookh. Now
Edition, printed in Ruby Type; with the Preface and Notes from the collective edition of Moores Poetical Works, and a Frontispiece from a Design by Kenny Meadows.

32mo. 2s. 60.–An Edition in 16mo. with Vignette, 5s.; or 12s. 6d. morocco by Hayday.

Moores Lalla Rookh. A New

Edition, with numerous Illustrations from original Designs by John Ten- Niel, engraved on Wood by the Brothers Dalziel. Fcp. 4to.

(In preparation,

Moores Irish Melodies. A New

Edition, with 13 highly-finished Steel Plates, from Original Designs by eminent Artists. Square crown 8vo. 21s. cloth; or 31s. 6d. bound in morocco.

Moores Irish Melodies, printed in Ruby Type; with the Preface and Notes from the collective edition of Moores Poetical Works, the Advertisements originally prefixed, and a Portrait of the Author. 32mo. 2s. 6d. An Edition in 16mo. with Vignette, 5s.; or 12s. 6d, morocco by Hayday.

Moores Irish Melodies. Illustrated by D. Maclise, R. A. New Edition; with 161 Designs, and the whole of the Letterpress engraved on Steel, by F. P. Becker. Super-royal 8vo. 31s. 6d. boards; or 2.12s. 6d. morocco.

Moores Irish Melodies, the

Music, namely, the Symphonies and Accompaniments by Sir John Stevbn-soif and Sir Hhhrt Bishop, printed with the Words. Imperial 8vo. 31s. 6d. cloth; or 42s. half-bound in morocco.

The Harmonised Airs from

Moores Irish Melodies, aa originally arranged for Two, Three, or Four Voices, printed with the Words. Imp. 8vo. 16s. cloth; or 25s. half-bound in morocco.

Moores National Melodies, with

Music. National Airs and other Songs, now first collected. By Thomas Mooee. The Music, for Voice and Pianoforte, printed with the Words. Imp. 8vo. 31s. 6d. cloth; or 42s. half-bound in morocco.

M o o r e s Epicurean. New

Edition, with the Notes from the Collective Edition of Moores Poetical 12s. 6d. morocco by Hayday.

Morell.–Elements of Psychology: Part I., containing the Analysis of the Intellectual Powers. By J. D. Mokell, M. A., One of Her Majestys Inspectors of Schools. Post 8vo. 7s. 6d.

Morning Clouds. Second and cheaper Edition, revised throughout, and printed in a more convenient form. Fcp. 8vo. 5s.

Morton.–The Resources of Estates: A Treatise on the Agricultural Improvement and General Management of Landed Property. By John Lockhakt Morton, Civil and Agricultural Engineer; Author of Thirteen Highland and Agricultural Prize Essays. With 25 Lithographic Illustrations. Royal 8vo. 31s. 6d.

Moseleys Mechanical Principles of Engineering and Architecture. Second Edition, enlarged; with numerous Woodcuts. 8vo. 24s.

Memoirs and Letters of the late

Colonel Armine Mountain, Aide-de-Camp to the Queen, and Adjutant-General of Her Majestys Forces in India. Edited by Mrs. Mountain. Second Edition, Portrait. Fcp. 8vo. 6s.

Mure.–A Critical History of the

Language and Literature of Ancient Greece. By William Muee, of Caldwell. Vots. I. to III. 8vo. price S6s.; Vol. IV. 15s.; and Vol. V. 18s.

Murrays Encyclopaedia of Geography, comprising a complete Description of the Earth: Exhibiting its Relation to the Heavenly Bodies, its Physical Structure, the Natural History of each Country, and the Industry, Commerce, Political Institutions, and Civil, and Social State of All Nations. Second Edition; with 82 Maps, and upwards of 1,000 other Woodcuts. 8vo. 60s.

Murray.–French Finance and

Financiers under Louis the Fifteenth. By Jahss Mdbuy. 8vo. Id. 60.

ffeale.–The Closing Scene; or,

Christianity and Infidelity contracted in the Last Hours of Remarkable Persons. By the Rev. Ebseiitk -M. A. 2 vols. fcp. Svo. 6s. each.

Normanby (Marquis of).–A Year of lievolution. From a Journal kept in I aris in the Year 1848. By the Mabquis an Nobmanby, K. G. 2 vols. 8vo. 24s.

Ogilvie.–The Master-Builders

Plan: or, the Principles of Organic Architecture as indicated in the Typical Forms of Animals. IJv Geobge Ochlvib. m. d. Post 8vo. with7! Woodcuts, price 6s. 6d.

Oldacre.–The Last of the Old Squires. A Sketch. By Cbdbic Oldacbe, Esq., of Sax-Norinanbury. Crown 8vo. ys. 6d.

0shorn.–ftuedah; or, Stray

Leaves from a Journal in Malayan Waters. Bvcaptain Shbbabdosbobn, R. N., C. li. With a coloured Chart and tinted Illustrations. Post 8vo. 10s. 6d.

Osborn.–The Discovery of the

North-West Passage by H. M. S. Imes-tiaator, Captain R. MCLFBE, 1850-1854. Edited by Captain S Kebab n Osbobw, C. B. Second Edition, revised; with Portrait, Chart, and Illustrations. 8vo. price 15s.

Professor Owens Lectures on the Comparative Anatomy and Physiology of the Invertebrate Animals, delivered at the Royal College of Surgeons. Second Edition, with 235 Woodcuts. 8vo. 21s.

Professor Owens Lectures on the Comparative Anatomy and Physiology of the Vertebrate Animals, delivered at the Royal College of Surgeons i 1S44 and 1846. Vol. I. 8vo. 14s.

Memoirs of Admiral Parry, the

Arctic Navigator. By his Son, the Rev. E. Pabby, M. A., Domestic Chaplain to the Bishop of London. Fourth Edition; with a Portrait and coloured Chart of the North-West Passage. Fcp. 8vo. 5s.

Pattison.–The Earth and the

Word; or, Geology for Bible Students. By S. R. PATTIsoir, F. G. S. Fcp. 8vo. with coloured Map, Ss. 6U.

Dr. Fereiras Elements of Mate- ria Medica and Therapeutics. Third Edition, enlarged and unproved from the Authors Materials bv A. S. Tay Lob, M. D., and G. O. Bbbs, M. D. Vol. I. 8vo.!8s.; Vol. II. Part I. 21s.; Vol. II. Part II. 28s.

Dr, Fereiras Lectures on Polarised Light, together with a Lecture on the Microscope. 2d Edition, enlarged from the Authors Materials by Rev. B. Powell, M. A. Fcp. Svo. Woodcuts, price 7s.

Perry.–The Franks, from their
First Appearance in History to the Death of King Pepin. By Walteb C. Pebby, Barrister-at-Law. 8vo. 12s.6d.

Feschels Elements of Physics.
Translated from the German, with Notes, by B. Wist. With Diagrams and Woodcuts. 3 vols. fep. 8vo. 21s.

Fhillipss Elementary Introduction to Mineralogy. A New Edition, with extensive Alterations and Additions, bv H. J. Bbooee, F. R. S., F. G. S.; andw. H. MIlLKE. M. A., F. G. S. With numerous Woodcuts. Post 8vo. 18s.

Phillips.–A Guide to Geology.
By John Phillips, M. A., F. R. S., F. G. S., andc. Fourth Edition, corrected; with 4 Plates. Fcp. 8vo. 5s.

Phillips.–Figures and Descriptions of the Paleozoic Fossils of Cornwall, Devon, and West Somerset: observed in the course of the Ordnance Geological Survey of that District. By John" Phillips, F. R. S., F. O. S., 4c. 8vo. with 60 Plates, 9s.

Piesses Art of Perfumery, and
Methods of Obtaining the Odours of Plants; with Instructions for the Manufacture of Pet fumes for the Handkerchief, Scented Powders, Odorous Vinegars, Dentifrices, Pomatums, Cos-metiques, Perfumed Soap, andc.; and an Appendix on the Colours of Flowers, Artificial Fruit Essences, andc. Second Edition; Woodcuts. Crown 8vo. 8s. 6d.

Captain Portlocks Beport on the
Geology of the County of Londonderry, and of Parts of Tyrone and Fermanagh, examined and described under the Authority of the Master-General and Board of Oninance. 8vo. with 48 Plates, 24s.

Poxt-ell–Essays on the Spirit of the Inductive Philosophy, the Unity of Worlds, ana the Philosophy of Creation. By the Rev. Baden Powell, M. A., andc. Crown 8vo. Woodcuts, 12s. 6d.

Powell.–Christianity without
Judaism: A Second Series of Essays on the Unity of Worlds and of Nature. By the Rev. Baden Powell, SLA., andc. Crown 8vo. 7s, 6d.

Pycroft.–The Collegians Guide; or, Recollections of College Days: Setr ting forth the Advantages and Temptations of a University Education. By the Rev. J. Pycboft, B. A. Second Edition. Pep. 8vo. 6s.

Pycrofts Course of English
Readme; or, How and What to Read: Adapted to every taste and capacity. With Literary Anecdotes. Fcp. 8vo. 5s.

Pycrofts Cricket-Field; or, the
Science and History of the Game of Cricket. Second Edition; Plates and Woodcuts. Fcp. 8vo. 5s.

Quatrefages (A. De).–Rambles of a Naturalist on the Coasts of France, Spain, and Sicily. By A. De Qttatbe- Fages. Memb. Inst. Translated lty E. C. Otte. 2 vols. post 8vo. 15s.

Baikes (C.)–Notes on the Be-volt in the North-Western Provinces of India. By Chables Raiees, Judge of the Sudder Court, and late Civil Commissioner with Sir Colin Campbell. 8vo. 7s.6d.

Baikes (TO–Portion of the Journal kept by Thomas Raises, Esq., from 1831 to 1847: Comprising Reminiscences of Social and Political Life in London and Paris during that period. 2 vols. crown 8vo. price 12s.

Barey.–A Complete Treatise on the Science of Handling, Educating, and Taming all Horses; with a full and detailed Narrative of his Experience and Practice. By John S. Rabey, of Ohio, U. 8. In 1 vol. with numerous Illustrations. Just ready.

Dr. Beeces Medical Guide: Comprising a complete Modern Dispensatory and a Practical Treatise on the distinguishing Symptoms, Causes, Prevention, Cure, and Palliation of the Diseases incident to the Human Frame. Seventeenth Edition, corrected and enlarged by Dr. H. Reece. 8vo. 12s.

Beade.–The Poetical Works of
John Edmund Reade. New Edition, revised and corrected; with Additional Poems. 4 vole. fcp. 8vo. 20s.

Bees.–Personal Narrative of the Siege of Lucknow, from its commencement to its Relief by Sir Colin Campbell. By L. E. Reis, one of the surviving Defenders. Third Edition. Post 8vo. price 9s. 6d.

Richs Illustrated Companion to the Latin Dictionary and Greek Lexicon; Forming a Glossary of all the Words representing Visible Objects connected with the Arts, Manufactures, and Every-Day Life of the Ancients. With about 2,000 Woodcuts from the Antique. Post 8vo. 21s.

Richardson.–Fourteen Tears Experience of Cold Water: Its Uses and Abuses. By Captain M. Richabd-SOlf. Post 8vo. Woodcuts, 6s.

Horsemanship; or, the Art of
Riding and Managing a Horse, adapted to the Guidance of Ladies and Gentlemen on the Road and in the Field: With Instructions for Breaking-in Colts and Young Horses. Bv Captain Rich- Abdson, late of the 4th Light Dragoons. With 5 Plates. Square crown 8vo. 14s.

Household Prayers for Four
Weeks: With additional Prayers for Special Occasions. To which is added a Course of Scripture Reading for Every Day in the Year. By the Rev. J. E. Riddle, M. A. Crown 8vo. 3s. 6d.

Biddles Complete Latin-English and English-Latin Dictionary, for the use of Colleges and Schools. New Edition, revised and corrected. 8vo. 21s.

Riddles Diamond Latin-English
Dictionary. A Guide to the Meaning, Quality, and right Accentuation of Latin Classical Words. Royal 32mo. 4s.

Riddles Copious and Critical
Latin-English Lexicon, founded on the German-Latin Dictionaries of Dr. William Freund. Post 4to. 31s. 6d.

Biverss Rose-Amateurs Guide; containing ample Descriptions of all the fine leading variety of Roses, regu-larly classed, in their respective Families; their History and Mode of Culture. Sixth Edition. Fcp. 8vo. 8s. 6d.

Dr. E. Robinsons Greek and English Lexicon to the Greek Testament. A New Edition, revised and in great part re-written. 8vo. 18s.

Mr. Henry Rogerss Essays selected from Contributions to the Edinburgh Review. Second Edition, with Additions. 3 vols. fcp. 8vo. 21s.

Dr. Rogets Thesaurus of English Words and Phrases classified and arranged so aa to facilitate the Expression of Ideas and assist in Literary Composition. Fifth Edition, revised and improved. Crown 8vo. 10s. 6d.

Ronaldss Fly-Fishers Entomology: With coloured Representation of the Natural and Artificial Insects, and a few Observations and Instructions on Trout and Grayling Fishing. Fifth Edition; with 20 new-coloured Plates. 8vo. 14s.

Eowtons Debater: A Series of complete-Debates, Outlines of Debates, and Qnestions for Discussion; with ample References to the best Sources of Information. Fcp. 8vo. 6s.

Dr. C. W. Russells Life of Cardinal Mezzofanti; With an Introductory Memoir of eminent Linguists, Ancient and Modem. With Portrait and Facsimiles. 8vo.12s.

The Saints our Example. By the Author of Letters to my Unknown Friends, andc. Fcp. 8vo. 7s.

Scherzer.–Travels in the Free States of Central America: Nicaragua, Honduras, and San Salvador. By Dr. Carl Scherzer. 2 vols. post 8vo. 16s.

Schimmelpenninck (Mrs.)–

Life of Mary Anne Schimmelpenninck, Author of Select Memoirs of Port Roj1al and other Works. Edited by her relation, Christiana C. Hankin. 2 vols. post 8vo. with Portrait, 15s.

Dr. L. Schmitzs History of

Greece, from the Earliest Times to the Taking of Corinth by the Romans, K. c. 146, mainly based upon Uishop Thirl-walls History. Fifth Edition, with Nine new Supplementary Chapters on the Civilisation, Religion, Literature, and Arts of the Ancient Greeks, contributed by C. H. Watson, M. A. Trin. Coll. Camb.; also a Map of Athens and 137 Woodcuts designed by G. Scharf, jun., F. S. A. 12mo. 7s. 6d.

Scoffem (Dr.–Projectile Weapons of War and Explosive Compounds.   By J. Scopfhen, M. B. Lond., late Professor of Chemistry in the Alders-pate College of Medicine. Third Edition. Post 8vo. Woodcuts, 8s. 6d.

Scrivenors History of the Iron

Trade, from the Earliest Records to the Present Period. 8vo. 10s. 6d.

Sir Edward Seawards Narrative of his Shipwreck, and consequent Discovery of certain Islands in the Caribbean Sea. 2 vols. post 8vo. 21s.

The Sermon in the Mount.

Printed by C. Whittingham, uniformly with the Thumb Bible. 6imo. Is. 6d.

Sewell (Miss).–New Edition of the Tales and Stories of the Author of Amy Herbert, in 9 vols. crown 8vo. price 1.10s. cloth; or each work com-

Elete m one volume, sparately as fol- Jwb :–

AMY HERBERT 2s. 6d.

GERTRUDE 2s. 6d.

The EARLS DAUGHTER. 2s. 6d. The EXPERIENCE of LIFE. 2s. 6d.

CLEVE HALL 3s. 6d.

IVORS, or the Two Cousins 3s. 6d. KATHARINE ASHTON.3s. 6d. MAR-
GARET PERCIVAL.5s. Od. LANETON PARSONAGE.4s. 6d. By the same
Author, New Editiom,

Ursula: A Tale of English Country Life. 2 vola. fcp. 8vo. 12s.

Readings for every Day in Lent:

Compiled from the Writings of Bishop Jeeemy Tayloe, Fcp. 8vo. 5s.

Readings for a Month preparatory to Confirmation: Compiled from the Works of
Writers of the Early and of the English Church. Fcp. 8vo. 4s.

Bowdlers Family Shakspeare: In which nothing is added to the Original Text; but
those words and expressions are omitted which cannot with propriety be read aloud.
Illustrated with 36 Woodcut Vignettes. The Library Edition, in One Volume, medium
8vo. price 21s.; a Pocket Edition, in 6 vols. fcp. 8vo. price 6s. each.

Sharps New British Gazetteer, or Topographical Dictionary of the British Islands
and narrow Seas: Comprising concise Descriptions of about 60,000 Places, Seats,
Natural Features, and Objects of Note, founded on the best authorities. 2 vols. 8vo.
2.16s.

Short Whist; its Eise, Progress, and Laws: With Observations to make any one
a Whist-Player. Containing also the Laws of Piquet, Cassiiio, Ecartt, Cribbage,
Backgammon. By Major A. New Edition; with Precepts for Tyros, by Mrs. B. Fcp;
8vo. 3s.

Sinclair.–The Journey of Life.

By Cathebine Sinclaib, Author of Tlte Business of Life. Fcp. 8vo. 5s.

Sir Boger Be Coverley. From the Spectator. With Notes and Illustrations, by W.
Henby Wills ; and 12 Wood Engravings from Designs by F. Taylee. Crown 8vo. 10s.
6d.; or 21s. in morocco by Hayday.

The Sketches: Three Tales. By the Authors of Amy Herbert, The Old Mans Home,
and Hatckttone. Fcp. 8vo. price 4s. 6d.

Sinees Elements of Electro-Metallurgy. Third Edition, revised; with Electrotypes
and numerous Woodcuts. Post 8vo. 10s. 6d.

Smith (G.)–History of Wes- leyan Methodism. By Geobge Smith, F. A. S., Author
of Sacred Amalt, andc. Vol. I. Wesley and his Times; Vol. II. The Middle Age of
Method-urn, from 1781 to 1816. Crown 8vo. 10s. 6d. each.

Smith (G. V.)–The Prophecies relating to Nineveh and the Assyrians. Translated
from the Hebrew, with Historical Introductions and Notes, exhibiting the principal
Results of the recent Discoveries. By Geobge Vance Smith, B. A. Post Svo. 10s. 6d.

Smith (J.)–The Voyage and

Shipwreck of St. Paul: With Dissertations on the Life and Writings of St. Luke,
and the Ships and Navigation of the Ancients. By Jakes Smith, F. E. S. With Charts,
Views, and Woodcuts. Crown 8vo. 8s. 6d.

A Memoir of the Bev. Sydney Smith. By his Daughter, Lady Hol Land. With a
Selection from his Letters, edited by Mrs. Austin. New Edition. 2 vols. 8vo. 28s.

The Eev. Sydney Smiths Miscellaneous Works: Including his Contributions to The Edinburgh Review Three Editions:– 1. A Libbjlhy Edition (the Fourth, in 3 vols. 8vo. with Portrait, 36s.

2. Complete in One Volume, with For.

traitand Vignette. Squarecrown,8? o. 21s. cloth; or 30s. bound in calf.

3. Another Nett Edition, in 3 vols. fcp.

8vo.21l.

The Eev. Sydney Smiths Elementary Sketches of Moral Philosophv, delivered at the Royal Institution in the Years ISM to 1806. Fcp. 8vo. 7s.

Snow.–Two Years Cruise off

Tierra del Fuego, the Falkland Islands, Patagonia, and in the River Plate: A Narrative of Life in the Southern Seas. By W. Pabeeb Snow, late Commander or the Mission Yacht Allen Gardiner. With Charts and Illustrations. 2 vols. post 8vo. 24s.

Bpbert Southeys Complete Poetical Works; containingall the Authors last Introductions and Notes. The JAbrary Edition, complete in One Volume, with Portraits and Vignette. Medium 8vo. 21s. cloth; 42s. DOund in morocco.–Also, the First collected Edition, in 10 vols. fcp. 8vo. with Portrait and 19 Vignettes, price 35s.

The Life and Correspondence of the late Robert Southey. Edited by his Son, the Rev. C. C. Southey, M. A. With Portraits, andc. 6 vols. post 8vo. price 63s.

Southeys Doctor, complete in

One Volume. Edited by the Rev. J. W. Wasteb, B. D. With Portrait, Vignette, Bust, and coloured Plate. Square crown 8vo. 216.

Southeys Life of Wesley; and

Rise and Progress of Methodism. Fourth Edition, edited by Eev. C. C. Southey, M. A. 2 vols. crown 8vo. 12s.

Spencer.–Essays, Scientific, Political, and Speculative. By Hebbebt Spenceb, Author of Social Statics. Reprinted chiefly from Quarterly Reviews. 8vo. 12s. cloth.

Spencer.–The Principles of Psychology. By Hebbbbt Spenceb, Author of Soda! Statics. 8vo. 10s.

Stephen.–Lectures on the History of France. By the Right Hon. Sir James Stephen, K. C. B., LL. D. Third Edition. 2 vols. 8vo. 24s.

Stephen.–Essays in Ecclesiastical Biography; from The Edinburgh Review. By the Eight Hon. Sir James Stephen, K. C. B., LL. D.

Third Edition. 2 vols. 8vo. 24s.

Stonehenge.–The Dog in Health and Disease: Comprising the various Modes of Breaking and using him for Hunting, Coursing, Shooting, andc.: and including the Points or Characteristics of Toy Dogs. By Stonehenge. 8vo. with numerous Illustrations.

In the press.

Stonehenge.–The Greyhound:

Being a Treatise on the Art of Breeding, Rearing, and Training Greyhounds for Public Running; their Diseases and Treatment: Containing also Rules for the Management of Coursing Meetings, and for the Decision of Courses. By Si u-.; in-, i. i. With Frontispiece and Woodcuts. Square crown 8vo. 2ls.

Stows Training System, Moral

Training School, and Normal Seminary for preparing Schoolmasters and Governesses. Tenth Edition; Plates and Woodcuts. Post 8vo. 6s.

Strickland.–Lives of the Qneens of England. By Agnes Strickland. Dedicated, by express permission, to Her Majesty. Embellished with Portraits ot tvory Queen, engraved from the most authentic sources. Complete in 8 vols. post 8vo. 7s. 6d. each.

Memoirs of the Life and Services of Rear-Admiral Sir William Symonds, late Surveyor of the Navy. Edited by J. A. Shakp. 8vo. with Illustrations, price 21s.

Taylor.–Loyola: and Jesuitism in its Rudiments. By Isaac Tayloe. Post 8vo. Medallion, 10s. 6d.

Taylor.–Wesley and Methodism. By Isaac Taylor. Post 8vo. Portrait, 10s. 6d.

Thackers Coursers Annual Remembrancer and Stud-Book: Being an Alphabetical Return of the Running at all Public Coursing Clubs in England, Ireland, and Scotland, for the Season 1857-8; with the Pediyrees (as far as received) of the Dogs. By Roeert Aekam Welsh, Liverpool. 8vo. 21s.

Published annually in October.

Bishop Thirlwalts History of

Greece. Library Edition; with Maps. 8 vols. 8vo. 3.–An Edition in 8 vols. Icp. Hvo. with Vignette Titles, 28s.

Thomsons Seasons. Edited by

Bolton Coeney, Esq. Illustrated with 77 fine Wood Engravings from Designs by Members of the Etching Club. Square crown 8vo. 21s. cloth; or 36s. bound in morocco.

Thomson (the Rev. Dr.)–An

Outline of the necessarv Laws of Thought: A Treatise on Pure and Applied Logic. By William Thomson, 1). D. New Edition. Fop. 8vo. 7s. 6d.

Thomsons Tables of Interest, at Three, Four, Four-and-a-Half, and Five per Cent,, from One Pound to Ten Thousand, and from 1 to 365 Days, in a regular progression of single Days; with Interest at all the above Rates, from One to Twelve Months, and from One to Ten Years. Also, numerous other Tables of Exchange, Time, and Discounts. New Edition. 12mo. Se.

The Thumb Bible; or, Verbum

Sempiternum. By J. Tayloe. Being an Epitome of the Old and New Testaments in English Verse. Reprinted from the Edition of 1693. 61mo. ls.6d.

Tighe and Davis.–Annals of

Windsor; Bcinga History of the Castle and Town: With some account of Eton and Places adjacent. By R. R. Tighe, Esq.; and,7. E. davis, Esq., Barrister-at-Law. With numerous Illustrations. 2 vole, royal 8vo. i. 4s.

Tooke.–History of Prices, and of the State of the Circulation, during the Nine Years from 18 8 to 1856 inclusive. Forming Vols, V. and VI. of Tookes History of Prices; and comprising a copious Index to the whole work. By Thomas Tooke, F. R. S. and William Newmaech. 2 vols. 8vo. 52s. 6d.

Townscml,–Modern State Trials revised and illustrated with Essays and Notes. By W. C. Towwsbrrd, Esq., M. A., Q. C. 2 vols. Svo. 30s.

Trollope.–Barohester Towers: a Novel. By Anthony Teollope. New and cheaper Edition,, complete in One Volume. Crown Svo. 5s.

Trollope.–The Warden. By Anthony Trollope. Po8t8vo.10s.6d.

The Travellers Library: A Collection of original Works well adapted for Travellers and Emigrants, for School-room Libraries, the Libraries of Mechanics In ttittttiona, Young Mens Libraries, the Libraries of Ships, and similar purposes. The separate volumes are suited for School Prises, Presents to Young People, and for general instruction and entertainment. The Series comprises fourteen of the most popular of Lord Macaulays Essays, and his Speeches on Parliamentary Reform. The department of Travels contains some account of eight of the principal countries of Europe, as well as travels in four districts of Africa, in four of America, and in three of Asia. Madame Pfeiffers first Journey round the World is included; and a general accountof the A "-fi-nlin, t Colonies. In Biography and History will be found Lord Ma-caulays Biographical Sketches of Warren Hastings, Clive, Pitt, Walpote, Bacon, and others; besides Memoirs of Wellington, Tu-renne, F. Arago, Ac.; an Essay on the Life and Genius of Thomas Fuller, with Selections from his Writings, by Mr. Henry Rogers; and a history of the Leipsic Campaign, by Mr. Gleig,–which is the only separate account of this remarkable campaign. Works of Fiction did not come within the plan of the Tbavellebs Libbaby; bat the Confessions of a Workins Man, bysau-vestre, which is indeed a fiction founded on fact, has been included, and has been read with unusual interest by many of the working classes, for whose use it ia especially recommended. Dumass story of the Maitte-darmes, though in form a work of notion, gives a striking picture of an episode in the history of Russi. Amongst the works on Science and Natural Philosophy, a general view of Creation is embodied in Dr. Kemps Natural History of Creation; and in his Indications of Instinct remarkable facts in natural history are collected. Dr. "Wilson has contributed a popular account of the Electric Telegraph. In the volumes on the Coal-fields, and on the Tin and other Mining Districts of Cornwall, is given an account of the mineral wealth of England, the habits and rrmnners of the miners, ana the scenery of the surrounding country. It only remains to add, that among the Miscellaneous Works are a Selection of the best Writings of the Rev. Sydney Smith; Lord Carlisles Lectures and Aildrcsses; an account of Mormonism, by the Rev. W. J. Conybeare; an exposition of Railway management and mismanagement by Mr. Herbert Spencer; an account of the Origin and Practice of Printing, by Mr. Stark; and an account of London, by Mr. MCulloch–To be had, in complete Sets only, at 5. 5s. pej Set, bound in cloth and lettered.

5S? The Travellers Library may also be nad as originally issued in 102 parts, Is. each, forming 50 vote. 2s. 6d. each; or any separate parts or volumes.

Sharon Turners Sacred History of the World, Philosophically considered, m a Series of Letters to a Son. 8 vols. post 8vo. 818. 6d.

Sharon Turners History of England during the Middle Ages-Comprising the Reigns from the Norman Conquest to the Accession of Henry VIII. 4 vols. 8vo. 50s.

Sharon Turners History of the

Anglo-Saxons, from theearliest Period to the Norman Conquest. 3 vols. 36e.

Dr. Turtons Manual of the Land and Fresh-Water Shells of Great Britain: With Figures of each of the kinds. New Edition, with Additions by Dr. J. E. Gbay, F. R. S., andc., Keeper of the Zoological Collection in the British Museum. Crown 8vo. with 12 coloured Plates, price 15s. cloth.

Dr. Ures Dictionary of Arts,

Manufactures, and Mines: Containing a clear Exposition of their Principles and Practice. Fourth Edition, much enlarged. With nearly 1,600 Woodcuts. 2 vols. 8vo. 60s.

Uwins.–Memoir of Thomas

Uwins, R. A. Bymrs. Uwiws. With Letters to his Brothers during Seven Years spent in Italy; and Correspondence with the late Sir Thomas Lawrence, Sir C. L. Eastlake, A. E. Chalon, R. A., and other distinguished persons. 2 vols. post 8vo.

Van der Hoevens Handbook of

Zoology. Translated from the Second Dutch Edition by the Rev. William Clabe, M. D., F. R. S., Professor ot Anatomy in the University of Cambridge; with additional References by tne Author. 2 vols. 8vo. with 24 Plates of Figures, price 60s. cloth; or separately, Vol. I. Invertebrata, 30sM and Vol. II. Vertebrata, 80s.

Vehse.–Memoirs of the Court, Aristocracy, and Diplomacy of Austria. By Dr. E. Vehse. Translated from the German by Fbanz Demmleb. 2 vols. post 8vo. 21s.

Von Tempsky.–Mitla; or, Incidents and Personal Adventures on a Journey in Mexico, Guatemala, and Salvador in the Years 1853 to 1855: With Observations on the Modes of Life in those Countries. By G. F. Vos Tempsey, With numerous Dlustrations. 8vo. 18s.

NEW WORK8 PPBI. I8HBD BY LONGMAN AND CO.

Wade.–Englands Greatness: Its Rise and Progress In Government, Laws, Religion, and Social Life; Agriculture, Commerce, and Manufactures; Science, Literature and Arts, from the Earliest Period to the Peace of Paris. By JOHN Wade, Author of the Cabinet La eyer, andc. Post 8vo. 10s. 6d.

Wanderings in the Land of

Ham. By a Daughteb of Japhbt. Post 8vo. 8s. 6d.

Waterton.–Essays on Natural History, chiefly Ornithology. By C. Watebton, Esq. With an Autobiography of the Author, and Views of Waltonhall. 2 vols. fcp. 8vo. 5s. each.

Watertons Essays on Natural

History. Thibd Sebies ; with a Continuation of the Autobiography, and a Portrait of the Author. Fcp. 8vo. 6s.

Webster and Farkess Encyclopedia of Domestic Economy; comprising sxich subjects as are most immediately connected with Housekeeping: viz. The Construction of Do-mesticedioces. withthemodesofwann-ing. Ventilating, and Lighting them–A description of the various Articles of Furniture, with the Nature of their Materials–Duties of Servants–andc. With nearly 1,000 Woodcuts. 8vo. 50s.

Weld.–Vacations in Ireland.

By Chables Richabd Weld, Bar-rister-at-Law. Post 8vo. 10s. 6d.

Weld.–A Vacation Tour in the

United States and Canada. By C. R. Weld, Barrister. Poet 8vo. 10s. 6d.

West.–Leetuvcs on the Diseases of Infancy and Childhood. By Chables West, M. D., Physician to the Hospital for Sick Children; Physician-Accoucheur to. and Lecturer on Midwifery at, St. Bartholomews Hospital. 8vo. 14s.

Williehs Popular Tables for ascertaining the Value of Lifehold, Leasehold, and Church Property, Renewal Fines, andc. With numerous additional Tables–Chemical, Astronomical, Trigonometrical, Common and Hyperbolic Logarithms; Constants, Squares, Cubes, Roots, Reciprocals, andc. Fourth Edition. Post 8vo. 10s.

Wilmots Abridgment of Black-stones Commentaries on the Laws of England, in a series of Letters from a Father to his Daughter. 12mo. 6s. 64.

Wilsons Bryologia Britannica:
Containing the Mosses of Great Britain and Ireland systematically arranged and described according to the Method of Bruch and Schimper; with fil illustrative Plates. Being a New Edition, enlarged and altered, of the Jfjwcozo-ffia Britannica of Messrs. Hooker and Taylor. 8vo. 42s.; or, with the Plates coloured, price 4. 4s.

Yonge.–A New English-Greek
Lexicon: Containing all the Greek Words used by Writers of good authority. By C. D. Yonge, B. A. Second Edition, revised. Post 4to. 21s.

Yonges New Latin Gradus: Containing Every Word used by the Poets of good authority. For the use of Eton, Westminster, Winches ter, Harrow, and Rugby Schools: King s College, London; and Marlborough College. Fifth Edition. Post 8vo. 9s.; or, with Appendix of Eeithets, 12s.

Yonges School Edition of Horace.–Horace, with concise English Notes for Schools and Students. By the Rev. J. E. Yonge, Kings College, Cambridge; Assistant Master at Eton. Pabt I. Odes and Epodet, 12mo. 3s.; Pabt II. Satires and Epistles, 3. 6d.

Youatt.–The Horse. By William Youatt. With a Treatise of Draught. New Edition, with numerous Wood Engravings, from Designs by William Harvey. (Messrs. Long Man and Co. s Edition should be ordered.) 8vo. 10s.

Youatt.–The Dog. By William
Youatt. A New Edition; with numerous Engravings, from Designs by W. Harvey. 8vo. 6s.

Young.–The Christ of History:
An Argument grounded in the Facts of His Life on Earth. By John Young, LL. D. Second Edition. Post8vo.7s.6d.

Young.–The Mystery; or, Evil and God. By Johu Young, LL. D. Post 8vo. 7s. 6d.

Zumpts Grammar of the Latin
Language. Translated and adapted for the use of English Students by Dr. L. Schmitz, F. R. S. E.: With numerous Additions aud Corrections by the Author and Translator. 8vo. 14s.

. October 1358.
PBINTED BY SPOTTISWOODB AND CO., NEYT-STBBHT SQUABE, LON-DON.
MOORES MELODIES-EDITIONS PRINTED WITH THE Mix
MOO I NATIONAL MELODi:
BIBLIOIECA CENTRAL

A
I ./A.
ftnS

Lightning Source UK Ltd.
Milton Keynes UK
29 December 2010

164966UK00001B/190/P